PRAISE FOR TIED IN KNO

"Greg Willits is equal parts wisdom, experience, and humor. This book is a powerful reminder that we are not meant to let fear and worry rob us of our peace and joy, and that God is the only real solution to untying the knots in our lives." — *Pat Lencioni, best-selling business author and cofounder of The Amazing Parish Movement*

"My stomach is constantly messed up. Anxiety, insecurity, too much pizza ... you name it, I'm tied in knots. Thanks to Greg Willits's book, and maybe some Pepto-Bismol, I've got some relief." — *Lino Rulli, host of* The Catholic Guy *on SiriusXM's* The Catholic Channel

"Whether you're stressed beyond measure or trying to cope with and care for someone else whose stress is driving you crazy, Greg Willits has penned the perfect tool to help you reclaim your sanity and spiritual well-being. Full of practical strategies and doable spiritual wisdom, *Tied in Knots* isn't rocket science, but rather a common-sense companion for your journey to more peaceful living. Greg's honesty and wit make him the perfect ally as he shares his own life's struggles and triumphs with real-world perspective. Get busy untying the knots that are holding you back from giving God your best 'yes.'" — *Lisa M. Hendey, author of* The Grace of Yes *and founder of CatholicMom.com*

"Pope Francis has popularized his own personal devotion to Mary the Untier of Knots, a religious tradition that was established in Germany. Greg Willits's allusion to this Marian devotion in reference to our current need for peacemaking and harmony in our world is more than appropriate since the violent disruption of social harmony has all of us tied up in knots with doubts and fears for our future. His work is a source of helpful insights in loosening many of those fears." — *Archbishop Wilton D. Gregory, Archdiocese of Atlanta, Georgia*

"Only of late have I become more at ease with the knots of my life, and *Tied in Knots* has helped me continue that process, supported by the gracious prayers of the Mother of God. Retreat to a quiet place — knots and all — and slip between the covers of Greg Willits's simple but powerful reflection. Let God be God, and find deep, true peace." — *Bishop Robert P. Reed, president, The CatholicTV Network*

"No one gets out of this life unscathed or, as Greg Willits writes in this terrific book, without getting tangled in an occasional knot or two or three along the way. It's how we view those knots and how we go about unraveling them that makes all the difference. Drawing from his own school of hard knocks or, more specifically, shall we say 'hard knots,' combined with his extensive knowledge of the Catholic faith, Greg provides a beautiful but practical faith plan to help the reader deal with and learn from the big and small stresses in life. *Tied in Knots* is a reminder that no matter how tangled up we may feel in the end, those knots can, if we allow them, be powerful lessons that keep us more closely tied to Christ and his Church." — *Teresa Tomeo, best-selling Catholic author, host of EWTN's* Catholic Connection

"Greg Willits combines powerful personal insights with practical advice and spiritual resources to help people of faith find peace beyond all understanding. If you're stressed, you need to read this book." — *Dr. Greg Popcak, author of* God Help Me! This STRESS Is Driving Me Crazy!

"*Tied in Knots* is an engaging read. It not only outlines the greatest modern obstacles to joy and peace, it effectively reminds us that Christ's invitation to 'ask, seek, and knock' all require effort on our own part. A talented storyteller, Greg Willits borrows from real-life experiences and challenges, offering tangible and practical solutions to common problems. Greg lays out a battle plan for life, one that — if followed — will not only untie your knots but connect you far more deeply to the Lord, his Mother, and, ultimately, his Church. Drawing from the deepest wellsprings of Catholic prayer and devotion, the reader is given a tangible, achievable strategy to overcome the anxieties, stresses, and struggles that hold so many of us captive. A simple yet inspiring read, this book will help countless souls experience the peace God not only offers but promises to all those who seek him." — *Mark Hart, the Bible Geek*

"The devil hates this book. He'd much rather have you miserable and anxious and isolated from others. He has good reason to hate this book. That's why I know you'll love it. Don't settle for anything less than lasting peace — the kind you'll find with Greg Willits's guidance." — *Mike Aquilina, best-selling author and editor*

"In *Tied in Knots*, Greg Willits offers readers a vision of not only how to deal with stress and problematic situations but, more importantly, how to open oneself to the possibility of spiritual growth as we learn to recognize God's grace and presence even in life's most challenging moments." — *Amy Welborn, author of* The Catholic Woman's Book of Days

"Besides helping his wife and children get to heaven, part of Greg Willits's mission is to help others. With *Tied in Knots: Finding Peace in Today's World*, it's 'Mission Accomplished!'

Whether you have a few big knots in your life or just a lot of little ones, the practical wisdom and encouragement in this book will give you the tools to help untie them for good!" — *Gus Lloyd, host of* Seize the Day *on Sirius XM's* The Catholic Channel *and author of* A Minute in the Church

"None of us is immune to the struggles, crosses, and knots of life. This book is a spiritual essential that will give you the necessary strategies to rise above those challenges and find peace and hope in the midst of your trials. Inspiring!" — *Drew Mariani, nationally syndicated radio talk-show host and award-winning writer, producer, and director*

"In today's chaotic world, it is easy to lose our peace, yet hard to regain it. Jesus, the Prince of Peace, and Mary, our Queen of Peace, want us to share their true joy of experiencing more heaven on earth. Greg Willits does a beautiful job of leading us to the lasting peace that only comes from God." — *Tom Peterson, TV host, producer, and author of* Catholics Come Home

"In his new book, Greg Willits uses his no-nonsense approach to help us, at the very least, to loosen life's knots with stories and practical tips. He also reminds us how we got into this mess in the first place so that we can avoid getting life all tangled up again in the future. May your reading of this book bind you more closely to Jesus who frees you from all our entanglements!" — *Fr. Leo E. Patalinghug, TV and radio host, speaker, author, GraceBeforeMeals.com and TheTableFoundation.org*

"Greg Willits shares lots of insight into the worries and anxieties that plague us and leave us tied in knots. There are no quick fixes to those things troubling us, but Greg's everyman approach not only consoles but offers hope in tangible ways to help us reflect, pray, and surrender our suffering to God's will, and open ourselves to recognizing his abundant graces." — *Maria Morera Johnson, author of* Super Girls and Halos: My Companions on the Quest for Truth, Justice, and Heroic Virtue

"A marvelously personal, engaging, and inspiring look at all the knots and worries that so often consume us and frustrate our lives. Even better, Greg Willits offers helpful, real steps forward to the deep faith God calls us to." — *Allen Hunt, senior adviser at Dynamic Catholic*

"Greg Willits has long been one of my favorite Catholic writers and a great example to follow for how he thoughtfully and prayerfully engages in his faith and leads his family. I love his new book, *Tied in Knots,* and the powerful stories and lessons he shares to help us get rid of the various obstacles that negatively impact our faith, our health, and our relationships with our families. This is a road map of sorts that you will want to read and refer to again and again for the great wisdom it contains. If you are tied up in knots for any reason, or simply want to lead a happier, healthier, and more faith-filled life, this is the book for you!" — *Randy Hain, author of* Journey to Heaven: A Road Map for Catholic Men

"Peace. In this life, we all need it, but often it feels like a mirage in the desert, nice and shiny but, ultimately, unattainable. In *Tied in Knots,* Greg Willits points us to the true source of peace and allows us to drink living water that satisfies." — *Kevin Cotter, author of* A Year of Mercy with Pope Francis

"A comprehensive look at untying the knots in your life with practical advice in an engaging style." — *Jeff Miller, The Curt Jester, www.splendoroftruth.com/curtjester*

"*Tied in Knots* is the kind of book that meets you where you are. If you're stumbling and struggling, if you're unsure and seeking, if you're far along the path of mystagogy (and you know what that word means), you'll find a wealth of wisdom and insight. It is, hands-down, one of the best books I've read and is sure to become a classic." — *Sarah Reinhard, author and blogger, SnoringScholar.com*

"Being tied in knots is part of the human condition that we all experience. If you need a bit of practical help to untie one such knot, this book will help. If you need serious intervention to untie a few knots, this book will help. If you are desperately in need of a radical, supernatural transformation to untie countless deep-rooted and gnarly knots in your life, this book will help. Greg Willits is a brilliant storyteller, and the book you're about to read will change your life." — *Kevin Lowry from gratefulconvert.com, author of* How God Hauled Me Kicking and Screaming into the Catholic Church *and* Faith at Work: Finding Purpose Beyond the Paycheck

"In *Tied in Knots: Finding Peace in Today's World*, Greg Willits does what I wish all Catholic books would do: go beyond the theory and get into the practical messiness of our day-to-day life. Right off the bat I found myself jotting down notes of ideas and plans to start untying all the knots in my life, and you will too!" — *Tommy Tighe, author of* The Catholic Hipster Handbook, *host of SiriusXM's* The Chimney, *www.catholichipster.com*

TIED IN KNOTS

GREG WILLITS

Our Sunday Visitor

www.osv.com
Our Sunday Visitor Publishing Division
Our Sunday Visitor, Inc.
Huntington, Indiana 46750

Copyright © 2017 by Greg Willits. Published 2017.

22 21 20 19 18 17   1 2 3 4 5 6 7 8 9

Our Sunday Visitor Publishing Division
Our Sunday Visitor, Inc.
200 Noll Plaza
Huntington, IN 46750
1-800-348-2440

ISBN: 978-1-68192-105-1 (Inventory No. T1840)
eISBN: 978-1-68192-110-5
LCCN: 2016955215

Cover design: Tyler Ottinger
Cover art: Shutterstock; iStock Photo
Interior design: Dianne Nelson

PRINTED IN THE UNITED STATES OF AMERICA

About the Author

GREG WILLITS is the editorial director for Our Sunday Visitor and the author of *The New Evangelization and You: Be Not Afraid.* With his wife, Jennifer, he founded the New Evangelizers and Rosary Army apostolates, authored *The Catholics Next Door: Adventures in Imperfect Living,* and hosted "The Catholics Next Door" daily talk show on SiriusXM. In addition to raising their five children, Greg and Jennifer also chronicle their adventures in life, family, and ridiculousness in their weekly "Adventures in Imperfect Living" podcast at www.gregandjennifer.com.

DEDICATION

To my best friend, Jennifer.

And to our five incredible children:
Sam, Walter, Ben, Tom, and Lily.

Remember that God doesn't want you stressed. He
wants you to be joyful and full of hope in him. My
greatest hope and prayer is that you do what's
necessary to be untied from the knots of the world so
as to more fully experience the amazing lives and
vocations God has in store for you.

And in memory of Hector Alvarez, my incredible
father-in-law (FIL), who even in death played an
enormous role in the creation of this book.

Contents

"We learn the rope of life by untying its knots."
— Jean Toomer, poet and novelist

Know This

WHATEVER HAS YOU bundled up right now — loneliness, frustration, sadness, anxiety, regret, guilt, brokenness, loss, illness, family, work, lack of direction or purpose, or any of the other countless afflictions served with abundance in today's world — know *this* without a doubt:

That knot that has you all tied up may just turn out to be one of the greatest blessings in your life, and you *can* experience peace in your life once more, even in the midst of dealing with whatever has you tied in knots.

While I'll attempt to share techniques about how to untie various and assorted knots in life, the ultimate goal of this book, as the subtitle states, is to experience more peace in our daily lives — that is, true, deep peace — even in the midst of being tied in knots.

No matter the malady, there *is* hope, and peace, if you know where and how to look. Peace in today's world is possible. And, unbelievably, that knot you may be experiencing may be the very key to unlocking that peace.

So, let's unlock it.

Chapter One

Losing My Mind with Worry

*"I try not to worry about the future — so I take
each day just one anxiety attack at a time."*
— Tom Wilson, cartoonist

LILY GYLDENVAND WAS a round little woman with a
permanent smile, squinty eyes, and big glasses. She had
an affinity for pink polyester leisure suits and the same
short bobbed haircut that she wore year after year after
year. A wordsmith, she crafted books and articles and
letters, and, as editor of a Christian women's magazine,
pieced them together before those words made their
way into thousands of homes each month.

Her influence increased her reach, but never her
vanity, as she became a sought-after speaker, traveling
constantly to speaking engagements in between regular retreats into the basement of her small home on the
outskirts of St. Paul, Minnesota, where she painted and
knitted and crafted through multiple other creative endeavors.

The sister of my grandmother on my mother's side, Great-Aunt Lil was the first true artist I was to know in my life. She could do anything, it seemed, and was interested in everything. Quick to laugh and tell a story, she was a great woman and my first inspiration in my own early artistic pursuits. She traveled almost annually to visit our family wherever we moved to over the years, and was the only one to volunteer to take me to see *Superman II* in the movie theater when no one else wanted to go — even though she promptly fell asleep shortly after the opening credits. On top of all of this, Aunt Lil is solely responsible for introducing me to the wonders of peanut butter and bacon on toast. Don't knock it until you've tried it.

In line with her habit of perpetually writing, Aunt Lil prolifically wrote letters and postcards, keeping us perpetually up to date with her nonstop activities.

When I was in elementary school, Aunt Lil sent our family a postcard one summer day with a simple greeting: "Hope all is well for your clan," she wrote. "Excited to see you when you come to visit this summer. Weather has been nice lately. Miss you all."

It was a typical Aunt Lil postcard, written in her precise cursive script, neat and orderly, the obvious product of years of practice.

The next day another postcard arrived with an eerily similar greeting: "Hope all is well for your clan. Excited to see you when you come to visit this summer. Weather has been nice lately. Miss you all."

Nearly every day for the next several weeks, the same postcard greeting arrived in our mailbox.

Over the following years, as I progressed through high school and into college, Aunt Lil's brilliant mind slowly devolved into near incomprehension of daily events as Alzheimer's slipped in and ravaged her from within. When I last saw her while traveling through Minnesota in September 1988, my parents and I stopped to have lunch with her. Several times during our meal she'd turn to me, surprised to see someone sitting next to her, and ask, "And who are you?"

"I'm Greg, Aunt Lil," I answered her.

"My goodness!" she exclaimed. "How'd you get so tall?"

Minutes later she'd forgotten the conversation entirely, and once again was completely surprised to see me sitting in the seat next to her.

"And who are you?" she asked again.

A short time after, Aunt Lil slipped into unconsciousness before passing away.

Nearly twenty years later, my wife and I were running two nonprofit organizations full time. Two years prior I had left a career in the IT industry, where I had worked for more than ten years, in order to devote my time to producing various forms of new media. We had started a podcast in 2005 before Apple even offered podcasts on iTunes, and we were linking up with other people doing the same thing.

We also had an idea to start up a Catholic New Media Conference that would bring together Catholic bloggers and Catholic podcasters. We would gather people from various television and radio outlets, along with those from newspapers, magazines, and blogs, together for the first time: old and new media meeting together and talking about the future and collaborative opportunities in Catholic media.

I took on the entire onus of the project myself. My oldest sister, Nancy, and our good friend Maria Johnson helped with some of the logistics, but, for the most part, I decided I was going to do all of the prep work leading to the event. It was pride, perhaps, or an irrational need to control all elements of the event, to make sure everything went exactly as planned, but I trusted hardly anyone but myself to make it happen.

When I now think back on my lack of delegation and trying to do everything on my own, it was one of the worst decisions I ever made.

I created all of the signs, graphics, and websites. I managed all of the scheduling. I planned all the talks and workshops. I developed all the contracts for the speakers. I even made their plane reservations. I stuffed the goody bags and put them on the chairs. I signed up all the sponsors. I even designed the nametags for attendees. I did countless media interviews to try to bring people to the event. I planned to emcee the conference and deliver two different talks. I sprinted at a dizzying pace for weeks and months on end.

In the midst of the chaotic planning, my buddy Moose generously allowed me to take occupancy in his local coffeehouse, where I sat with papers and plans and contracts scattered around my computer alongside an ever-present coffee cup. I sat at the same table every day, working on my computer, making phone calls, plugging away at the overwhelming details of the conference.

Then one morning, as I began planning out my day, I realized that even though I could see on my calendar all of the phone calls, appointments, and meetings I apparently had conducted over the previous twenty-four hours, I had no actual memory of the day before.

I'm not just talking about an inability to remember what I had for dinner the night before, or what I'd watched on television. I'm saying I had *no* memories from the day before. I couldn't remember waking up, where I'd gone, or who I'd seen or spoken to. I couldn't remember if I'd done any of the things on my pages-long to-do list, or anything I had accomplished throughout the day. I couldn't remember anything. It was terrifying, like sinking into a black hole.

My mind was a complete blank space, as if everything had been erased, and I remembered Great-Aunt Lil and her repeated postcards that one summer, and how she had no memory of writing the card she'd sent the day before, or the day before that. Fear swept over me, that inkling of childhood knowledge that Alzheimer's is hereditary, and that maybe it had landed on me, though I wasn't even forty years old at the time.

So, I did the next wisest thing I could possibly do: I googled "early onset Alzheimer's."

Dr. Google assured me that, yes, indeed, I did have early onset Alzheimer's (and perhaps a fatal brain tumor, acne, and had suffered a stroke as well). But as I pored through all the information that may or may not have applied directly to me, I also discovered numerous and more relevant studies documenting the correlation between stress and myriad other health problems. Stress can worsen or increase the risk of conditions such as obesity, heart disease, Alzheimer's disease, diabetes, lupus, depression, gastrointestinal problems, and asthma, to mention only a few. In short, stress — so prevalent in our twenty-first-century society — can make you sick.

A Harris Poll done on behalf of the American Psychological Association claimed that 64 percent of adults in 2014 reported that financial worries were a significant source of stress, ranking higher than other major sources of stress: work was 60 percent; family responsibilities 47 percent; health concerns 46 percent. But those were just the tip of the iceberg.

We are all stressed. We're living in a world that wants us to be stressed. The world constantly provides new technology, new distractions, new commitments, and new worries to stress us out even more. If you're not stressed enough, let me send another notification to your phone. That not enough? Here's another social network to keep up with, along with a newsletter solicitation that you don't remember signing up for.

What causes stress? Again, looking to Dr. Google, stress can be caused simply by being sick, by relocating (which I've done more times in my life than I can recall without counting on my fingers and toes), change in marital status, a new baby, teenagers, children moving out of the house, a new job or unemployment, a death in the family, other family stresses such as an ill parent or child, emotional problems such as grief or guilt, and more and more.

By the time I had gotten through the multitude of self-diagnosis lists online, I wasn't as much worried about Alzheimer's anymore as I was about stress and my extreme lack of peace in my daily living.

So, I began to do some more research ... and it stressed me out even more! It may sound odd, but consider some hidden areas of stress in our lives, and the potpourri of random responsibilities and questions that ravage our brains each day and further rob us of much needed peace:

What are we going to have for dinner? Do I have enough hamburger to make chili? How much money is in the checking account? Can I afford to get the extra lean hamburger or not? Did I look to see if there was a coupon for ground beef? Or is there some already in the freezer? Oh, wait, was that a text? Do I need to answer it? Maybe I should, it could be important. Maybe tonight. No, wait. I promised the kids we'd watch the new superhero movie on Netflix. The electricity bill is due tomorrow. I can't forget that. Oh, look at what my cat is doing. I should take a picture of him and put it on Facebook. And I need to take a picture of this bowl of chili and post that, too. And while I'm at it I should check my RSS feed. That reminds me, we set the DVR for Shark Week and we should watch those shows so that we can erase them. I'd better check my email. And when is my next dentist appointment? I hope I don't need a crown, but that one tooth feels a little strange. I wonder if the dog is okay; she looked a little under the weather this morning. I better take her for a walk before she goes to the bathroom on the rug. Again. It's probably because she ate the garbage. Again. Oh no, I forgot to put the recycling out at the curb. Is it too late to have one of the kids do it? I should have one of the kids do it ... and so on and so on and so on.

Sound familiar? That constant mind chatter is enough to make anyone feel tied in knots, yet many of us live our lives that way every day. In some strange way, it seems that even the idea of giving something up can cause additional stress. Imagine giving up checking on email for a day, or not looking at social media for a week. How does that make you feel at this very moment? Maybe the mere idea of doing without something — for instance, not watching television tonight or giving up some other beloved thing — causes you a bit of consternation and stress.

In a world of twenty-four-hour news cycles; of constant buzzing, beeping, and notifications from our phones, watches, and computers; of uncertain futures in an unstable economy while our own bank accounts may sit depleted and fruitless; of watching family and friends amble purposelessly through life while we ourselves may struggle to find our own sense of purpose, the idea of peace may feel perpetually elusive.

I'm not talking world peace and an end to war, though that would, of course, be welcomed and wonderful. The peace we'll seek in these pages is the peace that allows you to sleep more soundly at night, to be more joyful from one day to the next, and to go comfortably through each moment without worrying (as much) about the next. There's no cure-all to avoiding stress, illness, brokenness, or difficulties in life, but there are concrete and achievable methods for experiencing great peace in the midst of all that life brings us.

And as we seek peace, as we try to manufacture some semblance of peace in moments of unrest, it may feel about as attainable as trying to grab hold of water as it pours through our fingertips and into the drain below. Often in our efforts to achieve peace, we create more unrest, more dissatisfaction, more frustration, and more anxiety as it slips further and further away.

Yet we chase after peace more fervently, often by seeking things that provide only momentary bursts of happiness: getaway vacations; expensive dinners out; binge-watching Netflix; pints of Ben and Jerry's (though my temptation is Graeter's Black Raspberry Chocolate Chip); overindulging in food, drink, or worse; seeking our base wants while inadvertently ignoring what we truly need.

We may fall prey to erroneous thinking, that if we can correct situations in life — if we can just find the right spouse, the right job, the right house, the right *thing* — then we'll have peace. If we could just fix that one problem, have that one thing — then we'd have peace.

Ironically, in my life, time and again, I experience the greatest levels of stress and pain when I take drastic measures to seek peace.

Conversely, my greatest levels of peace actually come when I deliberately stop taking drastic measures and instead learn to surrender to current circumstances. But how do you do that when lack of peace breeds anxiety and frustration, and even depression and despair?

In many ways, this is the crux of self-mastery and self-discipline: it is not a matter of doing violence to ourselves, but of controlling our passions so they don't control us. It is often when we allow our passions and desires to take root and to rule in our hearts that we experience the most unrest and lack of peace. Self-mastery allows us to experience true human freedom. And this freedom — true freedom — is what brings us true peace. We often lose peace when we lose control of our passions, when we allow our lives to get out of balance with worry, self-medication, overwork, or a myriad of other paths that take us away from doing the right thing.

When we govern ourselves, our passions, and our wants and desires, that's when we have truly lasting peace.

If you are experiencing a lack of peace in life right now, if you feel tied in knots, it's important before continuing to accept and acknowledge that finding peace does not usually happen all at once, and it usually doesn't come from achieving a specific goal. It comes as we take incremental steps toward learning how to have peace in all situations, even ones that normally cause stress.

Think of it this way: Try to recall a time in your life when you had a seemingly insurmountable task placed before you that would require huge amounts of energy (mental or physical), focus, stamina, or other resources. Perhaps you were challenged to run in a 5K event or even a marathon. Maybe you set about to write a novel or rebuild a car engine. Maybe you once strove to make the dean's list for several consecutive terms in school. Whatever it may be, there's probably a time in your life when you had a goal that at first seemed huge, but step by step you eventually reached that goal. Forget about any failures you may have experienced in life. For a moment, just recall and hold onto a moment where you actually experienced great success.

How did you feel in that moment as you wrote "The End" at the end of a book, ran that point-two of the 26.2 miles of a marathon, or whatever that major accomplishment was for you? How did it feel to be successful?

You didn't get there all at once, but by incremental steps. The diligence you put into the overall, long-term effort most likely yielded happiness, but you probably also felt deep contentment, a satisfaction that all of the sacrifices you made to get to that moment were all worth it. In fact, you could probably say that it was self-discipline, because you controlled your desire to goof off or do something else, which allowed you to reach that place of extreme satisfaction, contentment, and peace.

This is why when we control what we eat, get enough sleep, and strive for regular exercise we simply feel better. It is in mastering our appetites and fostering discipline, in reining in our desires for things that may not be good for us, in simply focusing on what is right, that we experience the right peace.

When we experience freedom from our passions and from the seemingly endless need to chase after "more, bigger, better" things in life, we find greater clarity in our daily lives. This makes it possible for us to direct our actions not only toward greater freedom and greater peace, but greater goodness in our own lives and the lives of others. When we're at peace — when we learn to be at peace and correctly seek peace in all circumstances — we're more capable of expressing love to others, of being better friends, of showing greater compassion and generosity. When we're at peace, we're happier with ourselves, more content to be who we were made to be as individuals, and more likely to express that individuality with confidence and joy. When we are free from the things in life that keep us captive, we can turn to seeking more good in the world and in the lives of others.

Returning to that situation years ago when I was planning that conference and literally thought I was losing my mind, it's easy in this nonstop world to get swept away in the chaos. I didn't have early onset Alzheimer's or any of the other scary diseases I found online. Instead, I was a victim of self-induced stress, of focusing on the wrong things, of not being willing to let the right things go, of not seeking peace, of embracing chaos.

Since that time, however, I've spent years seeking ways to have more peace in my life. I haven't always been successful (as my wife, friends, and family can attest), and even today my battle against lack of peace and severe unrest is a daily challenge. But my life is more purposeful, more meaningful, and more peaceful than it was all those years before. And I believe that what lies ahead in these pages are strategies that will help you find more peace in your life, too.

What you are about to experience in this book are techniques for untying the various and assorted knots in life — such as finding more time for family, hobbies, and prayer. At the same time, I hope this book will help you experience peace even as you face the often-unavoidable knots of illness, brokenness, and other trials that are beyond your control.

Keep in mind that while there is no one-size-fits-all solution, my hope is that through this book — where I will share my own personal and often ridiculous anecdotes of illness, unemployment, loneliness, and more — you'll find solace and joy through whatever darkness you may be experiencing and concrete remedies to experience peace despite pain.

This is not a book that provides surefire solutions for every situation. Even if I were a doctor, counselor, or pastor, that would be an impossible task. But as someone who has daily fought for more peace, I've been blessed to find it in many unexpected ways. I've also spent the better part of fifteen years creating media that impacts the lives of others in their own quests for more peace in life, and I believe that what you're about to encounter are practical first steps in your own journey for more peace.

In the upcoming chapters, I'll first share some quick fixes to help you take the first necessary steps toward a more peaceful daily existence. Then, using various anecdotes and observations, I'll show you some ongoing ways of finding more permanent joy in your life. And for the more difficult knots in your life, I'll provide time-tested techniques — both practical and prayerful — that can help you find peace in even the most difficult situations.

We may not always be able to put an accurate label on our struggles, but it is often in the course of the journey that we discover not only the source of our knots, but the ways to start untying them.

Thank you for joining me on this journey toward more peace. Now let's begin.

Chapter Two

Emergency Room

"You only have a few years to play this game and you can't play it if you're all tied up in knots."
— Willie Stargell, member of the Baseball Hall of Fame

IT WASN'T UNTIL I was about ten years old that my parents made me start wearing a seat belt in the car. In fact, I remember trips with my five older siblings where all of us lay splayed out in the back of our family station wagon. For longer trips we even had a nasty old mattress beset with stains from sources I'd rather not ponder which we would set over the folded-down seats.

But somewhere between the late 1970s and early '80s, my mother began collecting one horrible story after another about people who died in car accidents — but who would have survived had they been wearing a seat belt. And then someone within my mother's own circle of friends survived a wreck so monstrously horrific that she would surely have died had she not been wearing her seat belt at the time. That was it for Mom. After that, everywhere we went, we wore our seat belts.

In the years following, a shift occurred, spurred on by public-service announcements, billboards, and other cautious mothers, to the point where car manufacturers even created a seat belt that automatically fastened you in as soon as you shut the door.

After shattering my nose in a car accident when I was sixteen — even though I was wearing a seat belt — I became one of those stories of someone who could easily have been killed without a seat belt.

By the time I became a parent in the late 1990s, it had gotten to the point that when you installed a car seat (something I'm not sure my parents even owned when I was an infant), you could even go to the local fire station and they would check to make sure it was properly in place.

On a cross-country road trip in 2016, however, a seat belt nearly killed one of my children.

Because of the size of our family, we were driving through Iowa in a two-vehicle caravan. My wife and oldest son rode tandem in our second vehicle while I and our other four children took lead in a minivan. With one son in the passenger seat and two in the middle row, as I cruised down the highway at seventy miles an hour I happened to take a quick glance in the rearview mirror at my then seven-year-old daughter in the back right seat. Her eyes were wide with terror, and her hands were at her throat.

"I can't really breathe," she whispered when she saw my eyes meet hers.

I looked over my shoulder and saw that the middle seat's seat belt was somehow wrapped around Lily's neck. Knowing that seat belts may lock in place when you slam on the brakes, I flipped on my turn signal and came to a stop as fast — but safely — as I could, hoping the belt around my daughter's neck would not tighten in response to my pumping the brakes. My wife and son in the car behind me came to a stop as well, not knowing what was happening as I busted out from the driver's seat and ran for the back of the van. I flipped open the hatchback and leaned over the back seat where I discovered the extra seat belt was wrapped not once, but twice, around my daughter's neck.

To make matters worse, the belt was not a typical seat belt with a built-in release button, but was rather a belt permanently attached from the ceiling to the seat, which is then used as a regular seat belt when combined with a lap belt. At first glance, there was no easy way to simply release the belt to untangle our daughter.

"Stay calm," I told Lily, as I felt my own face going numb with panic. My wife told me later that she at first thought I was stopping for an emergency bathroom break for our dog, who was in the back of the van. But when she saw me moving so quickly, she knew something much worse had happened and, within moments, she was at the side of the van climbing in to keep Lily calm while I tried to figure out a way to release her from the constraints.

At first, I tried tilting Lily's neck backward so I could start to untwist the belt in a counterclockwise motion. But somehow, perplexingly, that only seemed to tighten the belt. I then tried to untwist it in the opposite direction, but that made it worse, and Lily's face started to turn blue.

Meanwhile, our then fourteen-year-old son Ben had taken off his eyeglasses and with the arm of the frames started poking at the seat belt's emergency release. Immediately, I understood what he was trying to do and, taking the glasses from his hands, poked futilely at the emergency release with the end of the temples, which were too thick to fit into the release.

Rushing back around the van I grabbed my car keys and ran back to Lily, begging God to save her, to loosen the belt, to release its grip. In a blur, I managed to grab just the right key that fit in the release button, and within seconds I was unwrapping the tightened belt from my daughter's neck.

As my wife swept Lily into her arms to calm the tears, I bent over with my hands on my knees and forced myself to breathe slowly as my entire body started to shake. My mind, however, was blinded with an explosion of "what ifs." What if I hadn't looked in the mirror when I had? What if I hadn't gotten the seat belt released? What if I had slammed too hard on the brakes and injured my daughter? What if? What if? What if?

And while my daughter was fine, though her throat did ache for the rest of the day, as we continued on our journey I kept thanking God for giving our son Ben such a simple idea. Such a simple solution. Like a miniature MacGyver, he was immediately prepared to use what was literally right in front of him to provide what should have been the most obvious answer.

Now, as the parents of four teenaged boys and a preteen daughter, our house is often rife with drama and the need for immediate fixes. Fortunately, we've only dealt with a handful of truly dangerous situations, but we've found that, like during that cross-country trip, when something unexpected storms in and threatens to steal the peace in our lives, there are often several immediate solutions that normalize situations and bring peace. Often these solutions are right in front of us, but because of the pain, stress, or worry that's so closely in front of us, we're blind to the most obvious — and easiest — solutions.

Chances are you picked up this book because you currently feel overwhelmed by something that is stealing your peace. As previously stated, we'll later dive into more concrete ways to handle tough situations that have us tied in knots, including an often miraculous, prayerful solution that has helped untie even the most troublesome of knots in many people's lives.

But before we get too deeply into those situations and solutions, I want to provide a handful of go-to "emergency room" solutions I've found that can immediately bring relief, provide clearheadedness, and allow you to breathe easier so you are better able to address the larger issues in your life. What follows are some proven methods for finding immediate peace as quickly as possible. Not all of these solutions are for everyone, but perhaps one or more of them may bring immediate relief from whatever may be troubling you right now.

I call some of these "Well, duh!" fixes, because when you read them, you may smack your forehead and say: "Well, duh! I already know this, I just haven't actually been doing it." Like my son's quick solution to freeing his sister from the seat belt, sometimes the best advice is the simplest and most obvious.

So, if you need a quick fix, I recommend you try one or all of these things just to provide some clarity and prompt peace so you can think straight again and begin to take steps forward to finding more permanent peace in your life.

HALT

Even for those of us fortunate enough not to have fought addiction, there is great wisdom in an acronym used by many people in recovery: HALT. It stands for *hunger, anger, loneliness, tiredness.*

And while some argue that addictions aren't trigger-based conditions, but rather ones that are constant and chronic (therefore, many people refer to themselves as being in "recovery"), the idea that certain emotions and conditions such as hunger or loneliness can affect our behavior still holds true whether you are dealing with an addiction or stress and a loss of peace.

Therefore, a quick emergency room device I've found that yields great results is to pause whenever stress or anxiety sinks in so I can briefly analyze whether I'm currently experiencing any of these symptoms.

Hunger

The one part of the HALT acronym that always gives me pause when I'm recommending it to others is hunger, simply because so many people already struggle with overeating. In fact, I'm certain someone picked up this book because he or she feels tied in knots over body appearance, eating habits, or even eating disorders.

So, don't be tempted to look at stress as an excuse for an extra candy bar or another bowl of ice cream. What I've personally found is that a full stomach will indeed help calm me down, but I don't need high-calorie or fatty foods to help me feel full. Instead, eating an entire cucumber or an apple often does the same trick. And one of the best quick fixes I've found to combat hunger that may have knocked me off balance is to eat a modest portion of something high in protein such as a protein bar (my favorite is the Pure Protein chocolate peanut bar with twenty grams of protein and only two hundred calories) or a skinless chicken breast followed by a tall glass of water.

Anger

Anger is a little trickier to handle, since it is an emotion with multiple facets. Remember, anger is not wrong in itself. But anger uncontrolled, unbridled, cultivated, and fanned is so bad it's rightly considered one of the seven deadly sins.

I've known people who live to be angry, as if anger is a source of power. Yet I can't think of a single time those same people were ever genuinely happy without it being at the expense of someone else.

Therefore, it's easy to see how anger — the power source of which is often paid for by other people — could eat away at peace in your life. By its very definition, anger cannot coexist with peace.

For me, anger is usually situational, caused when someone does something to offend me or cause me or my family undue harm — often this is righteous anger and not wrong in itself. Fortunately, I'm not prone to road rage or becoming overly angry on a regular basis, but when I do give into anger, it usually has vicious consequences that nearly always ends up hurting those around me. This is why the *Catechism of the Catholic Church* insists that when anger is "not controlled by reason or hardens into resentment and hate, [it] becomes one of the seven capital sins" (Glossary, p. 866).

So, what's the best way to counter anger? Philippians 4:4–7 (which I'll quote again later in this book) provides the most curious prescription:

Rejoice in the Lord always; again I will say, Rejoice. Let all men know your forbearance. The Lord is at hand. Have no anxiety about anything, but in everything by prayer and supplication with thanksgiving let your requests be made known to God. And the peace of God, which passes all understanding, will keep your hearts and your minds in Christ Jesus.

What a strange idea, to give thanks in all situations, both the good and the bad. What a completely countercultural suggestion, to give thanks when you're sad, or angry, or frustrated, or anxious, or stressed. I know not everyone reading this book has an active prayer life, or maybe you've never even developed belief in God or a relationship with Jesus Christ, but this is something that has been absolutely indispensable for me in my own quest for peace and happiness in life.

To me, I find the incredible promises made in these simple passages to be absolutely life-affirming: The Lord is near. The peace of God that surpasses all understanding will guard your heart and mind in Christ Jesus.

Imagine yourself at your angriest and then making the conscious decision to pause, to quiet yourself, and then with complete deliberation to utter the prayer: "I thank God for this difficulty that wants to steal away my peace and cause me anger. I thank God for this pain and ask for him to guard my heart and mind by replacing my anger with peace."

If anger has found a way to fester in your heart, the fastest way to eliminate it is to acknowledge the source of the anger, and to give God thanks for that difficulty with the confidence that he'll gladly take it away if you trust him to do so.

Loneliness

Over time, I've learned that I'm particularly susceptible to anxiousness when I'm overly hungry or tired. But as an introvert living in a house with a wife, five kids, a mother-in-law, a dog, two cats, and a rabbit, I'm not sure I even remember what loneliness is anymore! Still, I have extroverted children who, even if they're surrounded by family, experience the pangs of loneliness and may act out as a result, but will surprisingly improve their attitudes after just a few minutes of interaction with someone else.

The fact that it's possible to be lonely amidst a sea of people illustrates one of the trickiest aspects of loneliness. Loneliness really needs to be counteracted by direct and immediate interaction, so when we seek comfort and companionship primarily from social media (where it's not uncommon to have hundreds or even thousands of friends, fans, and followers) or even video chat, we come up empty.

If you're susceptible to bouts of loneliness that rob you of your peace, seek out opportunities to interact with other people in person. Look for ways to serve in your community or church as well as healthy places to spend time among other like-minded people, such as bookstores, gyms, or places where others are pursuing similar goals.

Tiredness

Being tired is one of my main sources of stress. Thankfully, I'm married to a wonderful woman who long ago figured out that when I take a ten- to thirty-minute power nap, it's akin to flipping a switch for me that nearly instantly fixes stress, depression, overwork, bad moods, and more. In fact, it's not uncommon for me to walk into our house after work, greet everyone, and retreat immediately to the bedroom to change clothes, set an alarm on my phone, and take a quick power nap before dinner.

Similarly, I've found that during times in my life where I pulled all-nighters to work on projects or simply to binge watch a television program, within a few days my body's natural rhythm is tossed around so violently that it becomes progressively more difficult to manage my mood, and then I'm even more prone to making bad eating and other negative behavioral choices.

WORK IT OUT

In late 2015, I hit my all-time highest weight of 262.5 pounds. Since I'm six feet five, I had convinced myself that my height helped hide the weight. But looking back at pictures from that time, it was obvious that even my XXL T-shirts were unable to hide what couldn't be hidden.

At the same time, I was enduring one of the most stressful and peace-stealing periods of employment in my entire adult life. I was frustrated, worried about my future, worried about my career, and generally unhappy each day as I walked into my office.

Facing the facts about my weight, I set about walking for forty-five to sixty minutes every day while simultaneously tracking everything I ate in a mobile and web app from LoseIt.com. After a few months, I managed to get back to under two hundred pounds, which hadn't happened since before my wife and I got married back in 1995.

But while I enjoyed tossing out all my fat clothes and reaping the benefits of sleeping better at night and generally feeling more energetic, what surprised me the most was how walking and lifting weights simply improved my mood. Though I often had difficulty beginning a workout, almost always within five minutes of doing so I'd feel happier, more relaxed, and even more confident.

Numerous studies point to a plethora of positive effects of even just twenty minutes of exercise each day. In my case, even though work was still difficult, I found that after just a few weeks my job was easier to handle every day when I'd walk before work. And if I had a particularly difficult day, my nights were always much improved when I'd go to the gym and lift weights for thirty minutes before heading home.

FEED THE BEAST

Similar to exercise, stress can be caused by junking up our systems with sugary foods and drinks, high fat-content snacks, and carb-loading on prepackaged foods.

While I'm far from being a health nut, I've learned from experience that I'm the most lethargic and unproductive — and therefore the most unhappy and frustrated — when I'm plowing through food without considering calories or nutrition.

I'm no dietitian, so the following is not meant to be a step-by-step guide for your meals, but the trick I've learned to maintain a proper blood sugar level (and thus desirable concentration and energy levels) is to eat mostly high-protein, low-carb, and low-calorie meals. In fact, nearly every morning for breakfast I either have a cup of Greek yogurt (usually under one hundred calories) or a couple eggs (fried, scrambled, or hard-boiled) with a large glass of water, and that easily tides me over for several hours. Then for lunch I eat one of the protein bars I mentioned above with another large glass of water, and, again, I'm fine until dinner. If I have a particularly busy or stressful day, or if I have a midday workout, I may treat myself to a second protein bar, a high-protein/low-calorie shake, or a piece of fruit, and it is amazing how well my mood and energy level can be sustained.

I strongly encourage you to find the diet plan that works best for your body type and lifestyle, and then stick with it. The long-term results are well worth it.

MEDICAL INTERVENTION

Back in 2007, I had been woken up several times over the course of several weeks with strange abdominal pressure that made it difficult to sleep.

Naively, I continued to ignore these symptoms, hoping they'd go away on their own, until I attended a much-needed weekend silent retreat. My gallbladder suddenly decided to quit working shortly after dinner on the second night of the retreat.

Overwhelmed by stomach cramps as the night progressed, I tried to distract myself with reading, pretending I wasn't in pain. Around 2:00 A.M., sweating profusely, I packed my bags and left a note for the retreat leaders that I was sick and had to head home.

Unfortunately, home was nearly two hours away, and I stupidly drove down the highway at sixty-five miles an hour, sleep-deprived and in pain, as cramps ripped across my abdomen and made it difficult to breathe. A mile from my house I had to pull over and vomit. Parched upon my arrival home, I walked into the house and drank some water, which I immediately threw up. I then collapsed onto the bed, telling my wife to call my mother to come watch our children, because she was going to need to take me to the hospital.

"We can't give you any pain medication until after we've done a CT scan," the attending doctor told me.

"Then let's do the scan!" I begged.

"But first you have to drink all of this," the doctor instructed as a nurse presented four large tumblers of chalky-tasting barium sulfate suspension, which would help the radiologists diagnose my malady.

"Every time he drinks something he throws it up," Jennifer told the doctor.

But with the pain so intense now that I was willing to do anything to make it stop, I sat up, channeled my inner college student beer guzzler, and downed all four cups before falling back onto the hospital bed and passing out. Shortly thereafter, while completely unconscious, I was wheeled into the CT scanning room and thereafter properly medicated for the pain.

Later that week, my gallbladder was finally removed.

The pain I endured over the course of those twelve hours was the worst I'd ever experienced. My female surgeon told me that what I went through was about the closest a man can ever get to experiencing what a woman endures during childbirth. If that's true, my wife is truly a superhero after birthing five not-so-small children.

Why am I telling this story?

Had I gone to the doctor at the sign of the first symptoms, all of that pain could very well have been avoided. For some, the same can be said of stress and anxiety. Yet, unfortunately, despite the number of legitimate medical cases, many choose to live in a perpetual state of anxiety rather than seek help.

According to the Anxiety and Depression Association of America and the National Institute of Mental Health, more than forty million adults in the United States are affected by various anxiety disorders.[1] That's nearly 18 percent of the population, yet only about one-third of those suffering from these highly treatable disorders actually seek treatment.

For some people, living in a perpetual state of stress and anxiety is a genuine medical condition, yet the stigma of mental illness and fear of the unknown often keep people from seeking medical help to alleviate stress that negatively affects daily living.

Just like I didn't cause my gallbladder to quit working, nor could I get it to work again on my own, for many people, anxiety is not their fault, and in many cases cannot be fixed by simple willpower.

Having had many friends and family members fight depression — often caused as a result of a generalized anxiety disorder — and even losing a dear friend to suicide in 1989, I've become highly sensitized to the pervasiveness of mental illness. In many cases it is absolutely unnecessary for people to struggle with these issues.

---

[1] National Institute of Mental Health, "Any Anxiety Disorder Among Adults," https://222.nimh.nih.gov/health/statistics/ prevalence/any-anxiety-disorder-among-adults.shtml (accessed May 22, 2017); and Anxiety and Depression Association of America, "Facts & Statistics," https://www.adaa.org/about-adaa/ press-room/facts-statistics (accessed May 22, 2017).

I'm not necessarily recommending that the solution to all problems in life is to seek immediate medical intervention or counseling. But if you deal with stress or anxiety that makes it difficult to engage in work, school, social or activities (particularly activities you once enjoyed), or if you find yourself restrained by a phobia or inability to stop worrying, it might be worth the effort to talk to a doctor and at least explore the possibility of getting medical assistance.

Just think about it. If you contracted a virus, you'd see a doctor. If you broke a bone, you'd see a doctor. Anxiety and depression can develop over time due to a chemical imbalance in the brain. If you're dealing with ongoing stress from known or unknown sources, it might be worth exploring this with a medical professional.

PRAYER AND MEDITATION

Years ago, when I was a software-development manager in the information technology industry, my life was often so hectic and harried that every day at lunch I'd retreat from the office and sit quietly in my car for thirty minutes of prayerful silence. Doing this for months on end, I never stopped being amazed at how peaceful and relaxed my afternoons were once I committed to this practice.

For years, multiple sources such as the American Heart Association, Johns Hopkins, JAMA Internal

Medicine, and others have repeatedly highlighted the myriad health benefits of even a few brief minutes of meditation each day. These perks include decreased blood pressure, lowered depression and anxiety, relief from chronic pain, and better sleep.[2]

I can testify to all of these benefits at one time or another in my life. In fact, nearly every time I go to a doctor's office and have my blood pressure checked, the nurse will inevitably ask, "Is your blood pressure always this good?"

While to some, meditation can be as simple as slowing your breathing and calming your mind, I personally need more than that. As I've previously alluded, my relationship with Jesus Christ is at the forefront of bringing more peace into my life in the world today, and it is in ongoing conversation with God throughout my days that I find the greatest peace. On days when I fail to maintain this conversation, I often experience the most strife.

It's tempting to think that prayer has to be a complex and burdensome task, but God hears us even in our simplest pleas. While there are days when my prayer is much more robust with flowery vocabulary, I've learned

---

2 Dr. Nina Radcliff, "Health and the art of meditation," *The Washington Times*, January 6, 2017, http://www.washingtontimes .com/news/2017/jan/6/health-benefits-meditation (accessed May 31, 2017).

that monosyllabic prayer is often just as good as extreme experiments in verbosity.

In fact, I've often joked that I pray like Cookie Monster: "Greg need help. God help Greg."

More often, when I'm in stressful situations, I may utter other simple prayers throughout the day such as, "Lord Jesus Christ, son of God, have mercy upon me, a sinner." Or even more simply, just saying, "Jesus Christ" several times in a non-blasphemous way can bring deep peace from the Prince of Peace.

EMERGENCY ROOM CHECKOUT

This is only a very high level list of ideas to relieve stress in the short term. I present all of these not only as ideas you may want to consider, but also to encourage you to think about healthy and quick methods you may have employed in your own life that have helped overcome your own lack of peace.

We'll dive into more detail on several of these in later chapters.

Chapter Three

Unwrapping Gifts

"We look at life from the backside of the tapestry.
And most of the time, what we see is loose threads,
tangled knots."
— John Piper, founder of DesiringGod.org

MY MOTHER ALWAYS PLACED our wrapped presents in plain sight under the Christmas tree during the weeks of Advent leading up to the big day. I have no doubt she took great joy in tormenting her children, knowing that as soon as we walked through the door after a day at school, we'd scan under the tree for new packages, even though we knew it would be weeks before we could open them.

As soon as she left the room, I'd cautiously crawl amidst the boxes looking for ones with my name on the label. When I found a new one, I'd try to guess its contents from the weight, the size, how much it rattled, or how solid it felt. Over the years, I learned that my mother was a master gift wrapper. Socks would be shoved into empty Ritz cracker boxes. A boxed set of books would be first wrapped in a towel. Star Wars action figures were always covered in bubble wrap.

No matter how hard I tried, I could rarely guess what was hidden in the wrapping. I always knew what I desperately hoped for, and many times I received that very thing, but often I was surprised with the unexpected, receiving a boxed set of books my mother had caught me looking at months before even though I hadn't asked for it, or unwrapping the Star Wars Hoth Battleset that I never even dared to ask for. Often, the best Christmas blessings were the gifts I never would have requested, but which ended up being just the right ones for me.

No matter the size or shape of the wrapped box, I always believed something good was inside. And even if it ended up being something as mundane as underwear, there was something about the anticipation and waiting that had occurred that made me appreciate it regardless.

The knots in our lives can be kind of like that. Sometimes we just have to live with a particular knot for a time, until it works out and we can see the blessing that's been wrapped up inside it all along.

As I write this book, there are several knots in my life that revolve around things that won't come to fruition for quite some time. I have the knot of trying to meet deadlines for this very book that you now hold in your hands. I have the knot of wondering if it will truly help people as much as I hope it will. I have the knot of needing to wake up at 5:00 A.M. every morning to try to write out a few hundred words before heading into work. (That you're reading this book tells you I met my deadline, or that I was given yet another reprieve ... so that's one set of knots taken care of.)

My wife and I are facing an uncertain financial future as we inch toward our fifties with no substantial retirement plan in place. I'll be honest, I worry that I'm going to be working nonstop the rest of my life until I drop dead. Some of our older children are dealing with various difficulties that we, as parents, wish we could take care of for them. Instead, we can only watch as they learn how to navigate the waters of young adulthood on their own.

Still, facing these knots (or whatever knots you're dealing with in your life), what good does it do to stress out about them? To indulge in sleepless nights or allow worry to manifest so deeply that it begins to affect relationships and the way we treat others?

How can I instead look at each of these knots and see a blessing that could come from them? To see each knot, each difficulty, as an opportunity to improve myself and improve the lives of others? Before we can entertain that question, though, let's take a moment to understand what a blessing truly is, versus what we sometimes think it is.

It's easy to think that a blessing should be a life-changing moment, such as an unexpected financial windfall, a new job, or a long-awaited answer to a prayer. But often our lives are filled with many smaller blessings that are easy to overlook and take for granted.

Like most words, the definition is different depending on where you search for it. For example, one definition of blessing is simply something that brings about happiness or welfare. My children and my wife are a blessing to me merely by being in my life. I'm blessed to have a good job.

The *Catechism of the Catholic Church* goes further, however, and defines a blessing as more than just words uttered before diving into dinner or some simple nicety. Instead, it calls a blessing "a divine and life-giving action, the source of which is the Father; his blessing is both word and gift. When applied to man, the word 'blessing' means adoration and surrender to his Creator in thanksgiving" (1078).

Let's focus on that first part: "a divine and life-giving action."

How can something as mundane as a deadline bring about a divine and life-giving action?

More seriously, how can something as serious as abuse, depression, unemployment, betrayal, uncertainty, or fear bring about a divine and life-giving action?

For our purposes let's distill blessing down to its most basic: we seek good in our lives. And even in the midst of painful situations, good is possible.

At funerals, even while mourning the loss of loved ones, even as our hearts feel like they've been torn out and stomped on, we may suddenly find ourselves laughing until our stomachs hurt as we visit and reminisce with family and friends. I remember one moment at my father-in-law's funeral when two of our best friends, Mac and Katherine, came walking through the door. Just seeing them made me instantly start sobbing. But then just minutes later, Mac said some stupid thing that actually made me guffaw so loudly that people turned to look.

Again, even in the midst of pain, good is possible.

When we seek good in our lives, that alone is a life-giving action. That alone allows us to experience just a small taste of the goodness of God. Even if we don't actively seek out God as often or as well as we should in our day-to-day lives, we still instinctively seek out goodness. We seek the blessing of peace. We seek the blessing of grace and the certain knowledge that we're doing what we were made and intended to do. We want to believe that we are working *with* the circumstances of life for a greater good that benefits both us and those around us, particularly those we love and encounter on a daily basis such as our spouse, children, parents, siblings, relatives, coworkers, and friends.

Yet blessings don't always feel the way we think they should, at least not at first. In fact, sometimes we have to get through the challenges of the knots in our lives in order to be open to seeing and enjoying the blessings they hide.

Taking another cue from Catholicism, we can look at the practice of sacramentals. A sacramental is any action, object, or prayer that prepares a person to receive grace — in other words, to receive blessing — and to have the ability to cooperate with that blessing. The old Baltimore Catechism describes sacramentals as "anything set apart or blessed by the Church to excite good thoughts and to increase devotion." Any of those physical objects you immediately associate with Catholics — rosaries, holy cards, holy water, medals, statues — are examples of sacramentals. These are not superstitious good-luck charms. The *thing itself* does not bring the blessing, but it opens me up and prepares me to receive it. What actually brings the blessing is my disposition and prayers while using the sacramental.

In a similar way, any seemingly negative circumstance — any knot in your life — may be the very thing that is preparing you to receive grace and to better cooperate with it.

The difficulties you are wrestling with right now are like wrapped presents under the tree. You may not be able to see what gift is waiting in the midst of them. You may have to wait day after day and week after week — and maybe even longer — before the gift is revealed.

But the gift is real, and the knot you may be experiencing right now could be preparing you to better receive and cooperate with the gift that is waiting for you.

So ask yourself: What blessing may come from this knot? How is this knot preparing you to receive grace and to better cooperate with it?

It's a difficult question, but in the pages to follow we'll look at strategies for making it not only easier, but hopefully find a default response from you that will begin to lessen the knots that may plague your daily living.

ELEPHANT IN THE ROOM

Before continuing, it's important to address the elephant in the room that exists for so many people in today's world: the elephant of deep wounds.

In preceding sections, I shared with you some very personal hurts and difficulties. Yet even as I was outlining them, I was very cognizant that these hurts of mine are *nothing* compared to what haunts so many others. Maybe you carry some wounds so deep you can't even think about them. On the other hand, perhaps you're tempted to brush aside your own hurts because they seem too small and petty.

This isn't about comparison or a competition of woes. Your knots, your difficulties, both small and large, are unique to you. And your knots are extremely important because they are important to *you*, no matter how big or small they may seem. I believe completely that what I outline in later chapters will help you, no matter how difficult or even unimaginable your knots may be.

The truth is, there are some wounds along the ribbon of my life so difficult and deep and painful that I'm not going to print them in great detail. The details aren't necessary. Within my own life and that of friends and family I love deeply, tragedy of nearly every kind has reared its nasty head: abuse, suicide, adultery, divorce, addiction, abandonment, horrible sins, failure, poverty, and on and on.

As I write this, a lifelong friend is in surgery for a major procedure; my aunt is grieving the death of her husband just a week ago; and someone dear to me is suffering from a family member refusing to speak to her.

If you are dealing with a wound, whether deep or shallow, that has left you feeling particularly alone, I want you to know this book is especially for you.

Someone reading these words — maybe you — may be the victim of rape, abuse, or incest.

Someone reading these words — maybe you — may have had a relative murdered or unexpectedly killed by accident or illness.

Someone reading these words — maybe you — may still be reeling from the suicide of a loved one.

Someone reading these words — maybe you — may be harboring guilt from abortion or grievously hurting someone else.

Someone reading these words — maybe you — has been cheated on by a loved one, or perhaps has been the one to commit infidelity.

Someone reading these words — maybe you — may have committed some of the most unspeakably wrong acts you could imagine and desperately wants peace and forgiveness.

Even in the midst of these knots and worse, blessings are possible.

As we explore these difficulties and traumatic moments, or even the mundane, nagging knots that follow us like shadows, I encourage you to push forward.
Peace is possible in this world today, and peace is available to you.

Chapter Four

The Ribbon of Life

"What's got your wand in a knot?"
— Hermione Granger,
Harry Potter and the Goblet of Fire

MY RIGHT PINKIE FINGER would not stop convulsing from spasms as it repeatedly curled into a tight gnarl, then straightened, then contracted again, over and again a dozen times in rapid, involuntary succession.

I ignored it for weeks and even denied it was happening when one of my boys asked about it as we walked through the aisles of a local store.

"Why do you keep doing that with your finger?" Ben inquired.

"It's nothing," I muttered, and ushered him along.

"Your finger keeps twitching."

"It's nothing," I repeated while doubt cast a muddled shadow over my brain.

Was this some sort of late-stage epilepsy? Overactive neurons firing off in my brain, perhaps? Some other weird manifestation of stress and anxiety like my for-getfulness from years before?

I'd been aware of it, of course, but ignoring something so random is much easier than telling my wife about it, or, worse, making doctor's appointments and dredging through days in the uncomfortable awkwardness of waiting rooms, queued up at the ready to be poked and prodded in uncountable ways by strangers in white coats when, after all, it was probably nothing.

Besides, I could stop the twitching if I thought about it, forcing my finger to come to a standstill by staring at it like a Jedi mind trick. But it would do it again just moments later when I resumed whatever I'd been doing. I'd be watching television, and the next thing I knew it was twitching again. I'd be sitting in the pew during Mass, and it was twitching. Sitting in a meeting, with it twitching, I'd quickly move my hand underneath the table or shove it into my pocket.

Over the following few weeks, the minor little inconvenience moved up to my arm, causing spasms in my triceps and shoulder before traveling to my neck and finally moving into my face, at which point it became impossible to hide from others. It was beyond embarrassing to be in a conference room or engaged in water-cooler conversations that would be unexpectedly interrupted as my right eye would squeeze shut, my teeth grind together, my arm tense up, and my face contort into an uncontrollable grimace in rapid-fire succession.

Every few seconds I looked like a cartoon character who had just stuck his finger in a light socket.

"Sorry," I'd mutter. By this time, I had no choice but to admit to those closest to me that I was having a wee bit of a problem.

Though it was isolated to the right side of my body, I could not figure out what it was, and neither could a multitude of doctors. Soon I couldn't go more than two minutes — literally — without a significant spasm on the right side of my body.

The severity, strength, and repetitiveness got so bad that my wife was timing the spasms even as I was in deep slumber. Inevitably, I began to forecast worst-case scenarios.

"There's got to be a tumor the size of a grapefruit in my brain," I convinced myself. "There's some sort of mass that's infiltrated my nervous system through my spine. Maybe there's cancer in my spinal cord."

While a third neurologist ran me through the same regimen of examinations, she routinely popped a rubber reflex hammer on my left knee. It about knocked me off the table as my right side didn't just convulse, but spasmed with such ferocity that nothing I did could bring it under control for several seconds. I broke down sobbing as this doctor also was at an absolute loss as to a conclusive diagnosis.

The weeks slipped by in a stream of tests. I nearly vomited from stress in the hospital parking lot after having spasms within the claustrophobic confines of an MRI chamber. I trudged through lonely and fearful nights of mandatory sleep deprivation in advance of brain-wave tests. I choked down chalky-tasting liquids before a CAT scan. I fasted before ultrasounds and so many blood tests that I lost count.

Then there was the medicine, usually prescribed to epileptics, which helped just enough to give hope, but not enough to prevent the doctors from prescribing more and more and more, which led to an additional thirty pounds added to my already overweight frame. And with the prescription came depression so deep and oppressive that it made conversation nearly impossible at times, as all I could do was sit in darkness in the evenings, wrapped in a blanket sobbing and twitching and twitching and twitching. But I was afraid to admit my medically induced depression for fear that the medicine, which sometimes minimized my symptoms, would be taken away. It was impossible not to start imagining a life on disability insurance. My symptoms had progressed so rapidly that surely a time was not far off when I'd no longer be able to do my job.

In the meantime, all the tests continued to come back negative, and as the twitches increased, the multitude of doctors treating me would ramp up the dosage, expanding the darkness.

"I can handle physical ailments much better than psychological ones," I told my wife one night as I lay in bed, ravaged now more from the emotional wreckage of the medicine and misdiagnoses than from the original malady that began this dark season of my life.

I've always been able to handle physical ailments much easier than circumstantial doldrums. I'd welcome a broken bone over a broken heart, stitches over sadness. As often happens when a difficulty begins to consume life, it truly consumes. Like an oil spill, it seeps into relationships and turns normal conversations into cross-examinations, which causes withdrawal and loneliness. It turns restful nights into battles with darkness and unease, slapping at sheets and turning aimlessly until morning slams on the door and demands your attention through an insomnia-induced haze. Days become marathons of stumbling through the hours until it's time to crash back into bed and stare at the ceiling once again. In my case, my bad health was compounded by erroneously prescribed medication, which made me sluggish and lazy — which further made me think there was something wrong with me. I gained pound after pound after pound as my medicated laziness intensified.

Everywhere I turned, at every moment of each day, all I could focus on was this knot. And the more I focused on it, wanting it untied, the more tightly it bound upon itself, constricting and choking and demanding more attention so that it could tighten even more.

Knowing of my desperation for a solution as months passed and my symptoms continued, several people asked, "Have you gone to a chiropractor?"

The idea of opening myself to yet one more medical professional seemed like an exercise in additional futility. This was my new normal. This was my future. This was my forever. People didn't understand. And if I tried to make them understand, I just looked like a complainer. This was not something to just suck up and deal with, but no one understood that. People just saw me darkening, falling inward and away.

"We suspect this may be an immunodeficiency disorder," my primary neurologist at a local university hospital finally hypothesized. "Something called *facio-brachial dystonic seizures*."

"You suspect?"

"It's our best guess," she responded. "But we'll need a few more tests."

Desperately, I tossed out the suggestion that so many others had recently given me: "I was thinking of going to a chiropractor."

"Oh, no," she said and rolled her eyes. Then, without further explanation: "Don't do that. That won't be any help at all."

Instead, she suggested two other doctors to assist in treatment. There would be the possibility of other medications, of course. Yes, there would be some side effects, but wouldn't that be better than what I was dealing with? And surely it isn't as bad as you think it is, is it?

Having had my fill of medical referrals, one afternoon I went instead to a chiropractor I'd learned about at work. What would it hurt? And surely, at least, there wouldn't be additional prescriptions.

Like the earlier doctor who'd set me into seizures just by whacking my knee with a mallet, this new doctor directed me onto an examination table and, within five minutes of testing my mobility, accidentally managed to trigger one of my most violent bouts of twitches yet, literally forcing me off the table and onto a chair while I struggled to control myself.

"What the heck did you do?"

"Nothing," he said. "But I think I know what's wrong."

Over the next few weeks, the chiropractor did nothing more than treat me as he would a migraine patient, cracking my neck at first two to three times a week. As my symptoms decreased, so did my need for visits, down to once a week, and then once a month, and then once every several months.

Seemingly miraculously, I may now only have a brief twitch once every four to six months, and as soon as I do, a quick chiropractic adjustment always prevents further occurrences.

But for more than half a year my life was uncertain, fearful, tearful, and painful as I ballooned to over 260 pounds, as my relationships became fractured and frustrated, as I questioned God and myself and my job and my life choices.

Yet the tiniest thing — a five-minute visit to just the right person — set me on a path to recovery. When I stopped working against the knot and looked instead for a simple solution, the solution provided itself simply.

What might life have been like during those months of uncertainty and fear if, instead of worrying about what could go wrong as a result of my problems, I had concerned myself more with the potential mercy and blessings waiting for us each time adversity rears its ugly face?

Sometimes it's the easiest solutions, the ones right in front of our faces, that are the most difficult ones to see. And so are the blessings. But when we allow ourselves to look, often those simplest solutions are where we find the first signs of hope, and it's often in our weakest moments when we discover our greatest strength.

In all likelihood, you have your own memory of one or perhaps many times when unexpected or unwanted pain ravaged its way through the front door. You most likely have carried the weight of some sort of loss and pain that follows you like a shadow.

We all have these incidents in life, woven in and out — medical issues, lost loves, broken marriages, general dissatisfaction and lack of direction, addictions and struggles, unemployment, issues with our children, waiting for prayers that seem like they'll never be answered, seemingly uncontrollable thoughts and emotions, and tragedy upon sad tragedy.

In fact, as you read these words, one or more of these moments is likely drifting back to the surface.

For the purpose of this book, that's a good thing.

LOOKING BACK

What's a moment in your life — from childhood to pimply-faced adolescence to adulthood — in which the weight of struggles nearly made you buckle your knees from the pressure of it all? What's the memory that laid next to you like an unwanted and tear-inducing companion on sleepless nights? I want you to hold onto that memory, perhaps the strongest knot in your life, painful as it may be, for just a few moments more.

When I told one of my best friends that I was writing a book about finding peace and being untied from the anxious knots of life, he introduced a new knot for me.

"But you're the most stressed-out person I know," he accurately surmised.

It's true. Anxiety has had a way of tracking me down more accurately than Google Maps through a good portion of my life. Wherever I go, it seems to find me.

Nevertheless, I've realized — and come to accept — that I am very blessed in so many different ways.

My medical woes are nothing in comparison to others I know who have gone toe-to-toe against cancer, permanent disabilities, or system-ravaging diseases from which there is no return or remedy. Furthermore, I'm grateful that while I've experienced the loss of loved ones, I've never had to endure too many sudden, tragic deaths from unexpected accidents or illnesses. I have experienced unemployment, but I've always bounced back and ended up even better off after navigating through the tricky waters of looking for a new job.

As I said, I'm quite aware of my blessings.

But for me, those months of fighting the unknown malady that sent me into perpetual muscle spasms were a spotlight of discomfort, uncertainty, and fear of the unknown that will most likely track me the rest of my years. It is a daily decision not to be haunted by those events, and to choose instead to acknowledge the unexpected blessings that did, in fact, come from that trial. And while my particular medical experience might be unique, I know I'm not alone in being tied in knots from the side effects that accompany unexpected and stressful situations.

Growing up, I moved from Atlanta to Columbus, Ohio, to a small town in South Carolina (more on that later), then to the state of Florida, then Cincinnati, all within a few short years.

No kidding: by November of my sophomore year, I was already attending my fourth high school.

I added additional stress to my life when I set about graduating a year early. In my graduation class of nearly six hundred, I only knew one other classmate, and even that was merely on a cordial basis. In college I floundered further, waiting tables until one o'clock in the morning in an effort to pay my rent while still attempting to arrive in time for my 8:00 A.M. classes. That didn't work out too well.

By the time I got married at twenty-four, I'd already had more failed relationships, failed jobs, failed faith, and failed situations than I can honestly recall. Over the years I have dealt with bouts of various health issues, unstable and unsatisfying employment, parenting pitfalls, high-functioning autism diagnoses for two of my kids, financial hurdles, and more.

But here's the amazing thing from all of these years of struggles: from each difficulty I mentioned above, I can now point you back to a blessing that came from it. There's great truth in the often-overused adage "hindsight is 20/20": we see so much more clearly when we look back at our past.

What if you were able to start seeing more clearly looking forward? What if you were able to start seeing the potential blessings while currently caught in the trap, while standing in the midst of difficulties? I believe the more we are able to identify potential blessings that are to come from stressful "knots" that show up along the ribbon of our lives, the more easily we can get past the difficulties and the more peace we can experience, even in the midst of difficulties.

In grade school, you were most likely taught to diagram fiction stories or historical periods along a linear timeline. My own timeline would look a little like the one on the next page.

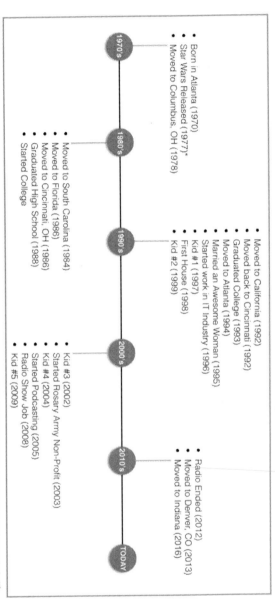

- Born in Atlanta (1970)
- Star Wars Released (1977)*
- Moved to Columbus, OH (1978)

1970's

- Moved to South Carolina (1984)
- Moved to Florida (1986)
- Moved to Cincinnati, OH (1986)
- Graduated High School (1988)
- Started College

1980's

- Moved to California (1992)
- Moved back to Cincinnati (1992)
- Graduated College (1993)
- Moved to Atlanta (1994)
- Married an Awesome Woman (1995)
- Started work in IT Industry (1996)
- Kid #1 (1997)
- First House (1998)
- Kid #2 (1999)

1990's

- Kid #3 (2002)
- Started Rosary Army Non-Profit (2003)
- Kid #4 (2004)
- Started Podcasting (2005)
- Radio Show Job (2008)
- Kid #5 (2009)

2000's

- Radio Ended (2012)
- Moved to Denver, CO (2013)
- Moved to Indiana (2016)

2010's

TODAY

* Embarrassingly important throughout my whole life

This is the *good* version of my life's timeline. It's humbling to admit that, if I'm completely honest, I often see more of the tragedy, difficulty, anxiety, and knots along the timeline of my life. In fact, it would be easier to draw a negative timeline of my life that highlighted the mistakes, foibles, sinfulness, pain, and brokenness than it was to draw out the more positive, simple outline you see.

How would you draw out the ribbon of your life? What do you most easily identify: the knots or the positive moments? What knot seems to have created the most significant snarl along the ribbon of your life?

Now, for each of your knots, can you identify a single blessing that has come from it? For example:

From broken relationships, or hurtful things people said or did to you: What people came to your aid and assistance? How have you perhaps been able to counsel others as a result of your own difficulties?

From unemployment: What new opportunities became available, or what new skills were you propelled to learn as a result of needing new work?

From health issues: Were you pulled deeper into prayer or reliance on others who showed you love? Were you inspired to take better care of yourself?

These are just a few examples of the blessings that may come from major events in our lives. Later, we'll look at how we can more easily see the potential for these blessings at the very outset of problems appearing in our lives, rather than waiting for hindsight to kick in after the fact.

Chapter Five

The Be Attitudes

"Why are you cast down, O my soul, / and why are you disquieted within me? / Hope in God; for I shall again praise him, / my savior and my God."
— Psalms 42:5–6

MY WIFE, JENNIFER, is blessed with the grace to quickly forgive, and even more quickly forget, when the events of life transpire against her. I, on the other hand, seemingly remember every nuance and detail, right down to time and date, of many of the difficult moments of my life.

I can tell you, for example, that at 10:18 P.M. on November 13, 1997, the episode of *ER* airing on television was the one in which the characters portrayed by George Clooney and Anthony Edwards were on a road trip. Who remembers this ridiculous kind of detail? Apparently, I do, and without even trying, because from that date and time, I can describe every detail of the hospital room my wife and I were in as a nurse suddenly rushed our newborn son to the neonatal intensive care unit. That's where he ended up spending his tenuous first days of life before finally being released to go home with us.

I can tell you exact dates when our radio show was canceled, and when I was laid off from another job several years before that. I can tell you the dates when we lost babies to miscarriage, and what time it was when my wife texted me to let me know her father died.

For every tragic or particularly chaotic moment in my life, I could bore you with all the humdrum details that surrounded it, most likely including what I ate for dinner that day. I'm not at all proud of this strange superpower. In fact, I highly suspect that others, perhaps even you, can recall with similar acuity the moments that are seminally important from your own life.

But it is this strange ability to recall past details that also sometimes leaves me feeling paralyzed with regret from past actions, past hurts, and past difficulties. It is for this reason that I'm often jealous of my wife's ability to so quickly forgive and forget. That's her amazing superpower, and it is indeed a gift.

Still, over years, I've learned a trick to deal with my frequent inability to let things go, and I believe it is key to untying the knots in our lives.

Looking at these moments along a timeline, discussed in the previous chapter, we can imagine our lives like a ribbon, fluid and moving. At birth, the ribbon is laid out flat and smoothly before us, with unknown and endless possibilities. As the years pass, however, and difficulties mount against us, knots begin to twist and form in the ribbon of our life, tangling us into balls of stress and worry. Time often allows knots to work themselves out as memories and emotional pain fade away, but some of these memories form worse knots that often grow tighter still as we wrestle against them.

In time, rather than working with a smooth ribbon, we begin working against ourselves, or perhaps against others.

But what if the knots in your life actually found their way there to *save* you? What if I told you that one of the best ways of finding peace with that knot is to stop trying to untie it?

Looking back, I can easily see the blessings that came from my most difficult situations:

I am SO GLAD I went through the heartache of painful breakups with girlfriends in my youth, because those lessons led me to realize what kind of woman I ultimately wanted to spend the rest of my life with.

I am SO GLAD I went through the various and many relocations of my youth, because it taught me fierce independence and self-reliance, and the ability to be nimble in quickly changing situations, which has time and again been such a huge blessing in my preposterously varied careers.

I am SO GLAD I had those health issues a few years ago, because it was a catalyst to finally taking control of my weight and exercise, and I ended up dropping more than sixty pounds and discovered the incredible stress relief of simply going for a walk several times a week.

While it's nice (and so much easier) to be able to see the blessings in hindsight, how much better would our lives be if we learned to see many of the blessings waiting to happen when we find ourselves embroiled in a knotty situation?

While it may seem completely backward and even counterintuitive to try imagining blessings coming from present difficult circumstances, this concept is not really anything new.

In fact, going as far back as the Gospel of Matthew we see eight specific examples of knots people may encounter in their lives, along with eight blessings that are promised to come from those knots. Note that the Bible doesn't suggest that these blessings *may* come from the difficulty, it says these blessings *will* come.

These eight difficulties and their companion blessings, commonly referred to as the beatitudes, are words of encouragement from Jesus Christ as he began proclaiming the Good News to the world:

"Blessed are the poor in spirit, for theirs is the kingdom of heaven.

"Blessed are those who mourn, for they shall be comforted.

"Blessed are the meek, for they shall inherit the earth.

"Blessed are those who hunger and thirst for righteousness, for they shall be satisfied.

"Blessed are the merciful, for they shall obtain mercy.

"Blessed are the pure in heart, for they shall see God.

"Blessed are the peacemakers, for they shall be called sons of God.

"Blessed are those who are persecuted for righteousness' sake, for theirs is the kingdom of heaven.

"Blessed are you when men revile you and persecute you and utter all kinds of evil against you falsely on my account. Rejoice and be glad, for your reward is great in heaven, for so men persecuted the prophets who were before you" (Mt 5:3–12).

Are any of the knots in your life right now reflected in the above statements?

For example, do you feel poor in spirit, perhaps distant from God or others, discouraged in life? Do you struggle with material poverty or financial worries? Do you feel as though the weight of the world is on your shoulders? Do you mourn the loss of a loved one, or perhaps the loss of status, employment, or some other situation in life? Is there some unanswered prayer that hangs around your neck like a noose?

As you read through the beatitudes, perhaps you can clearly identify with one or more of them. But even if your particular situation is not so clearly aligned in the beatitudes, the premise holds that there is benefit to first clearly identifying the knot troubling you, then focusing on the blessing the stress is pointing you toward, and then working forward from that place.

In other words, while we cannot predict the future, how might you take the knots in your life and develop a beatitude from them?

As we continue to work to untie the knots in our lives in future chapters, we'll dive more deeply into proactively seeing the blessings that could come from the knots currently in our lives.

How could this knot be of benefit to you? How could this knot be working to strengthen your character? Is there a weakness this knot is exposing so that you can become stronger, or perhaps simply learn to accept more completely? Is there someone else who may benefit from your knot? Is there someone who needs you to be a model as you suffer through your knot?

The beatitudes point us more firmly not to the problem or source of stress, but to the blessing. The poor in spirit will experience heaven. Those who mourn will be comforted. The meek will inherit the earth. The merciful will experience mercy. In untying the knots in our lives, we begin to experience peace when we focus not on the knot but on the potential blessings that knot may contain.

HOPE DOES NOT DISAPPOINT

Our knots and difficulties are often given to us to allow us to grow in the virtue of hope in God, and the ultimate joy he wants for us. It's easy to fall into the trap of thinking, "If only I had a different job, or different house, or different relationship, or more this, or more that, *then* things would be better."

Looking forward to these things can look and feel a lot like hope, but it is a misplaced and misguided hope that may actually cause even more knots. True hope is not just wishful thinking, but a theological virtue that allows us to "desire and expect from God both eternal life and the grace we need to attain it," according to the glossary in the *Catechism of the Catholic Church*. All real hope is directed toward something greater than the present moment, or even this present life. When we hope for the things we need at this moment, we hope for them precisely so that we can seek something even greater later in our lives.

Yet on far too many days of my life, I find the difficulties of daily living are stealing away my hope. Romans 5:1–2 says: "Therefore, since we are justified by faith, we have peace with God through our Lord Jesus Christ. Through him we have obtained access to this grace in which we stand, and we rejoice in our hope of sharing the glory of God."

Maybe you feel miserable at this moment. You may think you can't rejoice in the hope of sharing the glory of God because you can't even find the strength to seek out hope in him. Maybe you've been seeking hope in other people, in other things, in yourself, and in your circumstances. Don't give up — this same passage in Romans continues, providing a clear recipe for redirecting and aligning our hope: "More than that, we rejoice in our sufferings, knowing that suffering produces endurance, and endurance produces character, and character produces hope, and hope does not disappoint us, because God's love has been poured into our hearts through the Holy Spirit who has been given to us" (vv. 3–5).

Be encouraged. We do not need to expect immediate answers to the problems and knots in our lives, but we can have confidence that these problems and knots are leading us to something more.

Let's further break this down point by point:

1. We rejoice in our sufferings.
2. Know that suffering produces endurance.
3. Know that endurance produces character.
4. Know that character produces hope.
5. Know that hope does not disappoint, because God's love has been poured into our hearts through the Holy Spirit who has been given to us.

This is the straight pathway to achieve true hope in our lives. Even if you feel as though you are going through seemingly insurmountable difficulties at this very moment, and have no idea what to do about them, you can have hope. More than that, we can even rejoice in our sufferings and difficulties — whatever worries you're thinking of right now. And this rejoicing is one of the keys to finding the potential blessings in our various circumstances. But, as with so many aspects of our lives, this is so much easier said than done.

Why, then, would we rejoice in our sufferings?

Let's take a moment to evaluate what suffering may be.

When I first prepared to write this book, I surveyed the thousands of people who listen to the weekly podcast my wife and I produce, *Adventures in Imperfect Living* (available at gregandjennifer.com), and asked them what their biggest knots — or sufferings — are in life. I initially hypothesized that the sampling of responses I'd receive would fall into a few of the same categories, most likely in the scope of relationships, work, finances, and similar areas.

Instead, I received an overwhelming stack of emails where the suffering of so many people was more nuanced and not easily categorized. The responses I received included people suffering from:

- Fear of public speaking
- Frustration over people in parishes falling prey to the dictatorship of relativism
- Abusive relationships
- Custody battles
- Aging parents
- Strained relationships
- An inability to forgive someone
- Grown children or family who have abandoned their faith

- Pornography addiction
- Career changes
- Lack of self-esteem
- Inability to feel forgiven
- Feeling unworthy of love
- Aftermath of divorce and seeking an annulment
- Disappointment
- Difficulty trusting God's timing and plan
- Depression
- Overwork and lack of family time
- Fractured marriages
- Difficulty forgiving others
- General anxiety and stress
- School or work responsibilities
- Grief over loss of a loved one
- Political strife
- Lack of solid friendships
- Drug or alcohol addictions
- Terminal or chronic illness
- Financial issues
- Unemployment
- Anger
- Lack of family time
- Infertility
- Relocation
- Mental health issues
- False accusations
- Panic attacks
- Pride

- Same-sex attraction
- Technology addiction

And these are just a sampling of the responses!

Perhaps within these struggles, sufferings, thorns, and knots of others you see a reflection of your own difficulties in life. Perhaps you're thinking, "How do I possibly rejoice in any of these?"

Faith, by definition, is believing in something that cannot be seen. It is obviously much easier to rejoice and find happiness when we can actually see the good from a situation. Therefore, we need the faith to believe what we can't see: that our affliction is producing endurance, and from endurance there will be other fruits.

You might be thinking at this point: "Well, I've hit my margins when it comes to affliction. I'm good. I just want my current afflictions to be over with."

But endurance is important, and there's only one true way to build it up.

Think about when you've begun an exercise regimen, or if you've ever started a running program. Years ago, I didn't run at all, and then I was challenged to run a mile. That first mile was far more difficult than I could possibly have predicted.

But soon, by following a schedule, after several one-mile runs, I eventually moved up to three miles, and then five. Each of those miles was more difficult than the one before, and each mile came with unique challenges, but also a lot of learning. I learned that, for me, the second mile was always the most difficult as that is when my legs are prone to cramp. But if I pushed through mile two, then mile three and four and beyond became much easier.

In fact, after a few months of one-mile, three-mile, and five-mile runs, I was challenged to run nine miles, eleven miles, thirteen miles, and more. Eventually, I got to a point where I was actually relieved when I only had a five-mile-run day because that seemed so easy. Crazy, right? But because I had built up endurance, eventually I ran a full marathon and got 26.2 miles under my shoes. How did I do that? I'd built up endurance through the affliction of running.

Let's go back to Romans 5: If you build up endurance through difficulties, you will be better able to handle the troubles in your life. You may get to the point where you can say you are actually glad you went through that situation, maybe even glad you went through the pain of carrying around a difficult sin, or the painful burden of being hurt by someone else, because, somehow, by the grace of God, you are now a better person. You didn't like going through it, but having gone through it increased your endurance, and Romans 5 tells us endurance produces character.

What does that mean, exactly? Proven character is evidenced when you are truly living up to your identity of being made in the image and likeness of God. God gave you a particular character that is strengthened through endurance, which enables you to live a life for

God through every circumstance of every day. This is the lived definition of surrender.

God has given you this life, at this very moment, in this very place, with all the negative things that may have happened, and as we accept that we develop character. And that proven character produces *hope*.

Not hope in yourself — hope in *God*.

Remember what Romans 5:5 says: "And hope does not disappoint us, because God's love has been poured into our hearts through the Holy Spirit who has been given to us."

Think about this on a daily basis, especially when you're going through difficulties. Do you have hope right now? Do you have hope that God loves you? Do you have the hope that God cares so much about you that he gave you his Son? Do you have the hope that he wants you in heaven? Do you have the hope that he wants you to have a good life? If you are going through difficulties at this moment, you can have the hope that the affliction you are currently enduring could possibly be something that God has given you as a gift to produce greater endurance. Why? So that endurance will lead to the development of a greater character within you, and that that greater character can lead to an even stronger, greater hope in Jesus Christ.

I would suggest you write the first five verses of Romans 5 on an index card and carry it around with you. I did that for the longest time, pulling it out to read at moments of discouragement.

Use that card as a reminder of where to place your hope. In hoping for knots to be untied in our lives, or simply in hoping to be able to imagine a blessing that may come from those knots, too often we place our hope in ourselves, or in different circumstances, or we look for a different reality than the one we're actually living today. The true hope that will never disappoint invites us to look up, to rejoice, and to trust that God is working for our good even in the most challenging circumstances.

Chapter Six

Finding Joy Again

"All men and women are entrusted with the task of crafting their own life: in a certain sense, they are to make of it a work of art, a masterpiece."
— Saint John Paul II, Letter to Artists

ANOTHER ANTIDOTE to the many stresses we invite into our lives is simple: We need to discover joy again.

We are all incredibly busy, but sometimes our busyness isn't focused on the correct things. Our busyness robs us of happiness. It robs us of joy.

When you hear the phone buzz, or you get a text, or you see the new show that is on your Netflix queue, does that bring true joy? When you post a picture on Instagram of you deleting the show on the DVR that you just watched while eating the dinner you just made from the grocery shopping you just did based on the menu you just made and shared online, does this bring joy to your life? I'm willing to bet it doesn't. Perhaps there's a very temporary buzz of excitement, but it's a buzz void of long-lasting joy.

If we want to untie the knots and remove some of the stressors of life, we need to start working more on finding joy. We need to take active steps to seek out joy, rather than merely feeding the temporary happiness machine.

Before continuing, let's be clear on that difference: happiness and joy are not the same thing.

I went to a spiritual director years ago. In my first meeting, I told him: "Listen, I'm doing all of these things. I'm leading a Bible study at my workplace. I'm praying all the time. I'm doing everything I think God wants me to. But I'm just not happy."

He asked, "Yeah, but are you joyful?"

"What? No. I just told you that."

"No," he answered. "You said you aren't happy. I asked if you are joyful."

"I don't see the difference."

He went on, "Well, are you living in a state of grace?"

"I think so."

"You're going to confession?"

"Pretty frequently, yes."

"Are you going to Mass?"

"Of course."

"Are you living out your faith to the best of your ability?"

"I'm trying."

"Then you're joyful. You're doing what God wants of you. Be joyful."

"But I don't feel joyful."

"No. You don't feel *happy*. Be *joyful*."

What is joy? The *Catechism of the Catholic Church* places joy as one of "the fruits of the Spirit [that] are perfections that the Holy Spirit forms in us as the first fruits of eternal glory" (1832).

Happiness, conversely, can be the result of joy lived out, but a lower level of happiness can also be achieved by eating a bowl of ice cream. Happiness is often temporary and fleeting, whereas joy is pervasive and aligned with living a life of hope.

I struggled with the idea of happiness versus joy for years, and I'm pretty sure I could struggle with it for the next ten years, but the point is that although we seek happiness — the ultimate fulfillment of our vocation as children of God — we need to find joy, which is the fruit of the Holy Spirit that leads us to the eternal happiness that we really want.

So how do we find joy?

The short answer is that joy comes when you know you are walking in alignment with the will of God. Now, that sounds great, but it also leads ominously to bigger questions. If you are like me, now you may be asking, "What's the will of God for me?" And just when you think you have figured it out, circumstances change and suddenly you're asking the same question once again.

At times in our lives God's will may, in fact, entail doing big, heroic, courageous things. But often — I'd say most of the time — God's will for each of us is simply doing and living life as the person God made us to be, to honor our personalities, innate traits, and foibles.

God made you for a reason, even if sometimes that reason may not seem clear to you. He gave you certain talents, skills, and abilities. He gave you certain things that feed your soul, that won't feed someone else's. When you connect with those things, you will begin to connect with the joy that comes from being the person God made you to be.

LIVING WITH PURPOSE

When I was in the eighth grade, my English teacher, whom I stay in contact with to this day, pulled me aside after class and said, "Greg, you have no right, nor reason, not to be a writer." She arranged for me to be the only freshman in the journalism class at the high school the next year. When I was in college, I got a letter from her in the mail. I opened it up, and the note said, "Use this to advance your writing." Along with the note was an incredibly generous and unexpected check. I was a poor college student and it was a lot of money, but she saw something in me, so I set out to be a writer.

I wrote my first novel by the time I was twenty-three. It was terrible, so I destroyed every copy of it, but in 2000 I wrote another novel. I was positive that this was it, this was the one, this was the thing I was meant to do. I sent it out to have it published and promptly got rejected by more than one hundred fifty publishers and agents. I thought: "But I wrote this book, and I tried to make it moral, and I tried to make it good, and

I don't understand, because I thought I was writing this for God. I thought that I was doing the right thing, and I thought it was going to be something that was going to help the world." Every morning when I woke up, my first thought was that maybe *today* is the day I'm going to get that acceptance letter, and every night when I went to bed the last thought was that maybe tomorrow would be the day.

This went on for months, until my wife said one of the hardest things that's ever been said to me. It was one of the hardest, but also one of the most honest and loving things that anyone could ever say: "It sounds like you've turned that book into a god."

I said: "Well, then, forget about it. If I've turned this into an idol, then I'm done writing. I'm not going to have a god like that in my life." I stopped writing entirely. I just gave it all up. Maybe you can relate. Maybe you decided that you aren't going to do something even though you love it. Or maybe, less drastically, you have simply allowed something important to flitter out of your life.

Then, a few years ago, I read Saint John Paul II's Letter to Artists. In it, he said (and I'm paraphrasing): You artists, whether you're a writer, or a pianist, or a painter, whatever it might be, you are called to a special co-creation with God. He wants to share with you just a little bit of his creativity. The ultimate Creator wants to give that to you. Yeah, if you're chasing *The New York Times* bestseller list, maybe it ain't gonna work out for you, but if you're using this thing that God has given you, you are going to get to experience working in cooperation with God.

That teaching really hit me. Was I writing novels to cooperate with God's creativity or to see my name on a bestseller list? So, years after I gave up writing, I took that book that got rejected one hundred fifty times and started rewriting it from scratch, allowing myself to fall into the words with the mind-set of turning that craft of writing into a prayer and allowing God to work through this feeble person to do something greater and more personal, even if it was something that would be just between me and God.

I still would like it to make the bestseller list, but if it doesn't, it's okay, because I'm doing it not for fame and money, but to do my small part in sharing in God's creativity, which is something he wants to share with me. I'm doing it to cooperate with who God made me to be. It's been wonderful to do the thing that feeds me internally because God put that in me.

You experience joy when you understand who it is that God made *you* to be. As you develop a clear sense of your identity of self, your identity of family, and your identity of community, you begin to experience joy because God has a purpose for you — a purpose for you individually.

Often, in order to find our purpose, we first need to pursue something that stirs our passion, something we do just because we find it fun or satisfying. I think about a friend of mine, Gene Yang, who created the *Rosary Comic Book* as a result of his own passion for writing and drawing graphic novels. He was a high school computer-science teacher who wrote and drew comic books using his God-given gifts in a creative way. As soon as I discovered his *Rosary Comic Book*, I fell in love with it. The first panel for every mystery is a larger panel. That's the Our Father. Then he tells each mystery with ten smaller panels, so you literally can pray the Rosary without rosary beads just by using the comic book. Each of the individual panels tells the story of the mystery.

A few years later, Gene wrote a book called *American Born Chinese*, which was the first graphic novel ever to be awarded the Printz Award from the American Library Association. His writing career took off, and in 2015 he quit his job as a teacher because he is so busy working on comic books. Now he is the current author of the monthly *Superman* comic for DC Comics and was named the Library of Congress' National Ambassador for Young People's Literature. I think it's pretty cool that the guy who's writing *Superman* originally wrote and illustrated the *Rosary Comic Book*.

I told you about the *Rosary Comic Book* because the Rosary is one of my favorite prayers. And one of my favorite mysteries is the Wedding Feast of Cana. Gene draws Cana in the comic book showing Mary simply saying, "Jesus, they've run out of wine." And Jesus answers: "How is that any of our business, Mother? My time hasn't come yet." What I love about this story is that we're talking about God here. Here's this little Jewish woman who is going up to God and saying, "Jesus, they've run out of wine." Hint, hint. Wink, wink. Nudge, nudge. "Son, can you help them?" And what does Mary say to the servants when Jesus tells her his time has not yet come? The same thing she says to us: "Do whatever he tells you."

The next panel is my favorite in the entire comic book. After Mary tells them, "Do whatever he tells you," she gets out of the way, rushing off the page in a blur of motion, leaving Jesus with a blank expression. But then, what does Jesus do? He orders the jars filled with water and performs his first public miracle. Why? Because his mother asked. He acted at the behest and urging of his mom. If you think that Mary, Undoer of Knots, doesn't want to put you to work for her Son, if you think that she doesn't want you to do whatever he tells you to do, to really be untied, to experience true freedom, then I want you to reconsider. Mary wants us to trust her Son to act at her request. Through her, the knots of your life can be untied so that you can become servants, disciples in today's world.

But there's one more thing to consider: Christ often drew away from the crowds to pray. As it says in Luke 6:12, "In these days he went out to the hills to pray; and all night he continued in prayer to God."

When we seek to untie the knots of our lives, we must follow Jesus' example and allow God to pull us away from all the busyness of life, to pray, to hear from him, to let him show us what is causing us the greatest amount of stress. It might not be what we think on the surface, but if we ask God to reveal it to us, he will. And then we can take that stress, that knot, to his mother and ask her to intercede on our behalf and smooth it out of our lives forever. More on that later.

Chapter Seven

The Gift of Identity

"In fact, there are many knots that I cannot untie."
— Dwight Schrute, *The Office*

SOME MIGHT SAY my father-in-law, Hector, had questionable judgment, because when I asked for his daughter's hand in marriage, my only employment was playing guitar and singing (badly) for latte and tips in a coffeehouse. I didn't have a job and certainly not much of a future, yet he gave me his blessing to marry his daughter. But when he did, he looked me squarely in the eyes and said, "I trust you to take care of my daughter."

In June 2015, Hector started not doing so well. Over the previous few years he had dealt with multiple health problems, but now he had developed lung issues that the doctors struggled to diagnose and treat. "Well, you have bronchitis," they said at first. Then, a few days later, it was, "No, it's not bronchitis, you have pneumonia." Finally, with devastating clarity, they announced: "It's not pneumonia. It's cancer, and it's all in your lungs."

They at first assured us that he could still be around for quite some time, but just four days later, as we scrambled getting kids out the door during their first week of school, we received one of those terrible phone calls that almost takes the air out of the room and makes it feel as if the world just stopped turning. The doctors said very matter-of-factly that my wife needed to get on a plane right away because Hector only had twenty-four to forty-eight hours to live.

We rushed to pull the kids out of school, pack the van, and drop Jennifer off at the airport. Within three hours of that phone call I began the 1,400-mile drive back to Georgia with our five kids, hoping we'd get there in time. Around two in the morning, I ran out of steam and finally stopped at a hotel for the night. As the children and I were stumbling toward the elevator in the hotel lobby, I received a text from my wife.

"He's gone," she wrote.

She had arrived hours before, told Hector she loved him, and held her father's hand as he died.

At the funeral people got up and talked about Hector and what a great husband he was, and what a great father he was, and what a great grandfather he was. As I sat listening, I kept thinking: "No one knows there was more to him than that. No one is talking about what a great father-in-law Hector was."

No one knew of the inside jokes Hector and I shared. No one knew of the secret side glances we gave each other when our wives were talking, or that we signed emails to each other SIL and FIL (for son-in-law and father-in-law). No one knew that the only Spanish words I ever said to my Puerto Rican father-in-law were when I asked him if he wanted a *cerveza*, to which he'd usually answer, "*Sí, sí.*"

At his funeral, I was able to stand up and share with his friends and family that not only was Hector all the things they thought he was — husband, father, grandfather, brother, uncle, and friend — but in his life he became even more of what God meant for him to be, including father-in-law.

Hector didn't start out that way, though. Hector started as a single man, and he morphed into this new role of husband, and then he morphed from there into a new role of father. Then he further morphed into yet another unexplored role of father-in-law, and then into a new role of grandfather. His life, like ours, constantly evolved. But at the heart, there was always that part of Hector that remained constant, that part of him that was rooted in his core identity. Hector's outward roles may have changed, but part of him always was the single guy and the husband and the father and the father-in-law. It's true for Hector, and it's true for all of us. I will always have a part of that person I was thirty years ago. He makes up part of who I am now. But being married and being a husband, and being a father, and perhaps someday being a father-in-law and grandfather are part of it as well. It's one of the great mysteries of being human: We have our core identity of being a child of God, but we have these other roles as well, some of which are yet to be revealed.

The day after his death, I found a note that Hector wrote in his Bible. To me and those who loved him, his words have enormous poignancy: "Jesus Christ's death on the cross was the beginning of the promise of eternal life with him. In my heart and throughout my life should be a longing for that promise. Help me, Father, to continue to strive for eternal life in the way I live my life today. Thank you."

What a great treasure to find the day after he died. What a great identity to leave behind. I think Hector saw it fairly clearly. Hector was made in the image and likeness of God, and he strove to live as such. Did Hector make mistakes? Heck, yeah, he made mistakes. He never could fix that one cabinet door in our kitchen, for example, but he tried.

In each of his roles he had a different relationship. He had a different relationship with me, his son-in-law, than he did with his daughter-in-law. He had a different relationship with his son than he did with his daughter, whose hand he gave me in marriage. We all have roles that might be different from one relationship to the next, but they are still a part of who we are.

The First Letter to the Corinthians says, "Now you are the body of Christ and individually members of it" (12:27). Jeremiah 1:5 says, "Before I formed you in the womb I knew you," and still today, as Paul explained to the Corinthians, you are part of the body of Christ. Pay attention to those words.

You have importance in this world. You, as a child of God, are an intricate and needed part of the body of Christ. Just like a human body works best with two hands, ten fingers, and all other parts of the body, the body of Christ benefits from *you* being a part of it because God wanted you to be a part of it.

Therefore, we best serve the world and the entire body of Christ when we live in accordance with our fullest purpose, when we remove all obstacles that prevent us from living lives according to the will of God, which also means living lives of peace.

"Peace be with you," Jesus says in John 20:21. "As the Father has sent me, even so I send you."

When we're tied in knots, when we allow ourselves to keep living in a tangle of anxiety and sadness and frustration and dissatisfaction, when we don't turn that over for some major spiritual surgery, then we are living our lives pretending that we are not a part of the body of Christ.

Knots and anxiety steal away our peace and our ability to serve God and others to the fullest. Let's take back that peace and give it up to God.

CORE IDENTITY

Despite all my discussion of *doing* stuff, I want to stress this: It's absolutely necessary to discover your core identity, what God made you to *be*, and not to *do*. We have to know, deep down, who we are. We must know and respect and nurture our identity, as well as our roles.

Learning — and accepting — who we are at the base
of our identities is another key to untying that ribbon of
knots we carry around.

You may be wondering, at this point, how you
can get a clearer idea of who you are and what you are
meant to do. One way to do this is to take a chapter
from business books. Businesses often use something
called a value proposition. A value proposition makes a
company or product attractive to customers. So, what's
your value proposition?

The way to figure out your value proposition is to
start with a series of statements in which you fill in the
blanks.

I am a _____.

I help _____,

to achieve _____,

in order that _____.

I'll use one aspect of my identity as an example:

I am a storyteller.

I help others feel closer to God through writing, speaking, and other creative pursuits,

to achieve the goal of helping myself and others become
disciples,

in order that they can help other people in turn.

That's my value proposition.

How would you answer these questions? Take a few
minutes to think about this and perhaps even write it
down. Again, this helps you to put a definition on your
identity. It doesn't have to be just about your job. This
is an exercise you can do for all areas of your life. Think

about yourself as a person. Think about your core identity. Think about what God made you for. You might have put down the roles of spouse, parent, grandparent, but what's at your core?

Fill it in for yourself: "I am a _____. I help _____ to achieve _____ in order that _____." How about: I'm a disciple of God; I am a saint in the making; I am a writer; I am a husband; I am a father. I help my family to, hopefully, know God better, and, hopefully, I help other people to know God better, to achieve greater happiness here on this earth, greater joy on this earth in order that I can get to heaven, that my wife can get to heaven, that my children can get to heaven, and everyone else I can get to heaven is just gravy on top of the mashed potatoes.

How would you fill in the blanks?

What's your *true* identity? What are the core things that feed you, that shape you in the image and likeness of God, that form the version of you that you share with the world, but also the version of you that is more intimate and may only be shared with God?

I've moved around a lot throughout my life, and growing up as a kid I was blessed to have lived for two years in South Carolina. I made a ton of great friends there and still am friends with many of them. One of them was my buddy Eric — and after you read the following story, you may be surprised to learn is still a dear friend … and even more surprised that he still considers me as such!

Eric was one of the popular guys. All the girls thought he was one of the cutest things in the world, and when we were in the ninth grade, Eric had a girlfriend and convinced me to accompany him when he went for a visit. Because we lived in such a small town, we could walk everywhere. One ugly October, Southeastern Saturday night, we were walking back from his girlfriend's house and eventually found ourselves veering through the school parking lot.

One of my God-given personality traits is that I've always been convincing when I talk to people, even as a kid, and I've always had a way with words. As Eric and I were walking, I decided to put these two particular skills to work.

"Hey Eric," I said. "Let me ask you a question. If I tell you something, you promise that you won't repeat this to anybody?"

He answered, "Yeah, of course."

"You know what," I said, pausing dramatically. "Never mind."

"What is it?" Eric asked, his curiosity now raised.

"You can't tell anybody, Eric."

"Okay, what is it?"

"I'm serious."

"I won't," Eric insisted.

"Listen," I said, and waved my hands in front of me. I shook my head. "You know what? Forget it. I'm just messing with you, don't worry about it."

Now he was really curious.

"What were you going to say?" he asked.

"Well, okay, you swear you won't tell anybody?"

"I won't tell anyone. What is it?"

"I'm not messing around," I said. "You swear?"

"I swear."

I paused again, allowing an adequately uncomfortable silence to fall over us.

"Have you," I started, then paused again. "Have you ever flown before?"

"What are you talking about?" Eric asked. "Like in an airplane?"

I just shook my head: "You know what? Never mind."

Now I really had him: "Well, what are you talking about?"

"You swear you won't tell anybody?"

"I told you I won't tell!" Eric said, frustrated.

"Let me ask you, why do you think it is that maybe I'm kind of the goofy guy, I'm kind of the outcast, I hang out with the popular people, but I'm kind of … you know … hiding something. Maybe I'm trying to throw people off a little bit."

"What are you talking about?"

"Okay, you swear if I tell you something that you will never, ever tell anybody?"

"Yes! Of course, of course."

"Do you want to see something amazing?"

Eric stared at me, nearly afraid.

"Climb on my back and we'll fly," I told him.

"I'm not going to climb on your back," Eric said, and he laughed nervously.

I laughed along with him.

"I'm just messing with you," I said, and let another awkward silence fall between us, one that went for a minute, and then another.

We kept walking, and then Eric suddenly stopped and turned to me, trying to read my face.

"Okay," he said. "You fly first, and *then* I'll climb on your back."

"You idiot," I told him. "What's wrong with you? I can't fly!"

Twenty years later, I went to South Carolina to go fishing with my brother and called up Eric.

"Hey man," I said to him. "We're going to be fishing on the river. Why don't you grab your boat and join us?"

That evening my brother and I were off to the side of the river, and we were casting. Eric was in the middle of the river with his boat. He cast in and suddenly was fighting with his rod and reel. From the riverside I called over, "You got something?"

"No, it's caught on a snag," he called back.

I yelled over to him, "You need me to fly over there to help you out?"

Eric's been a great sport about my ribbing him about this since way back in 1985 and even gives himself a hard time now. In 2015, when my wife posted something kind about me on Facebook on our twentieth anniversary, Eric popped up and added, "And he can fly, too."

Now, I can't fly ...

... or, can I?

No, of course I can't fly. That's not what I was made for. I wasn't made to be a superhero no matter how many comic books I read. You weren't made to be a superhero either. You were made to be a *saint*, and that's infinitely — and eternally — better. Becoming a saint is our true identity. It's what we are meant to be.

What does that really mean, though, that you're called to be a saint?

When I think about saints, I think about people who did absolutely heroic things, people who would give up everything, such as Saint Francis of Assisi, who was from a wealthy family and gave up comfort and riches to live the poor life of a beggar. Or Saint Maximilian Kolbe, who offered up his own life for the sake of a father who was imprisoned along with his family in a World War II concentration camp.

I hear these stories and think, "How can I possibly do something like that?"

But our true identity demands openness to the will of God and trusting that if he indeed calls us to difficulties that he will supply the necessary graces not only to endure but to flourish.

If we can understand our identity, when we know who we truly are — not just, "Hi, I'm Greg, and this is my job," but who we are in the eyes of God — then we truly can see the possibility that sainthood is attainable. We can begin to recognize that, yes, it may seem unattainable at times, but we can work toward that sainthood, and we can want to be saints, because that is what God is calling us to be. When we have a clearer idea of what our identity is supposed to be, suddenly sainthood becomes more possible.

The Bible talks about our true identity. It is very clear about who you are. It gives a very clear definition of *your* identity: "God created man in his own image, in the image of God he created him; male and female he created them" (Gn 1:27).

The *Catechism of the Catholic Church* gives us a clearer idea of what this means: "Man occupies a unique place in creation: (I) he is 'in the image of God'; (II) in his own nature he unites the spiritual and material worlds; (III) he is created 'male and female'; (IV) God established him in his friendship" (355).

This tells us *exactly* who we are.

Look at the words from Genesis again: "God created man in his own image, in the image of God, he created him; male and female he created them." Humankind occupies a unique place in creation. We are made in the image of God, in his own nature. Now let's linger on this for a minute, because I think this is something that you can easily read but not always take in. Truly, what does this mean to you? Are you thinking: "Okay, fine, God created man in his own image. Adam, right? It only applies to Adam and Eve and those other folks from way, way back."

No. God created *you* in his own image, in the image of God. He created *you*, the very person who is reading these words.

Now you might be tempted to protest, "Oh, but I'm terrible, I'm a sinner, I'm a useless person, I'm no good." But God would say otherwise. Because God created you in his own image, he unites the spiritual — your heart, your soul — and the material, this fleshy substance, in *you*. God did that in you. He made you that way on purpose and for a purpose.

Listen to me carefully here: God did not make you to be tied up in knots and live a life of misery.

That is not why he made you.

If we act like we're not made in the image of God, and if we go about our daily existence thinking we're supposed to be tied up in knots and supposed to be miserable, we are not going to be able to do anything. It is then, I can guarantee you, that you're going to live a life of misery when you don't have to. Because this is not what you were made for. From the outset, God made you to be a saint, to be a disciple, and to know his love. He made you to be untied from knots.

Sometimes God shows us his love in unexpected or uncomfortable ways. For example, I'm not the most touchy-feely guy. If you ask me to go on a retreat, I'm going to ask you right back, "Is it a silent retreat where no one will talk to me?" Most people are surprised when they learn that I'm actually incredibly introverted, because I do radio and give talks and tend to be rather visible. Being introverted doesn't mean I'm shy; it just means that the way I'm energized, the way I'm refueled, is by alone time, by quiet time, by thinking time. I just need to sit and be still. Even so, I'd rather give a talk in front of ten thousand people than sit at a table with five other guys sharing personal stories.

But sometimes we have to be touchy-feely and a bit more outgoing, even when it's uncomfortable. One time, my wife, who's a little bit more touchy-feely than I am, called all of our children and me downstairs to our kitchen. All five kids came into the room and, of course, our dog came, too — after all, there's action going on in the kitchen.

Jennifer stood in front of me and put her hands on my shoulders and said, "Greg, you were made in the image and likeness of God, and I love you." It was a touchy-feely moment. In return, I put my hands on her shoulders and said, "Jennifer, you were made in the image and likeness of God, and I love you." We walked to our son, Sam, and put our hands on his shoulders and said, "Sam, you were made in the image and likeness of God, and we love you," and then he did the same to me and he did the same to his mom, and then we had the kids do it to one another. They kept going down the line until Walter, our then-fifteen-year-old, reached Ben, thirteen years old, and said, "Ben, you were made in the image and likeness of God, and I guess I love you."

Now, after we'd gone through the whole family, we looked down, and there's the dog at the end of the line, just knowing something's going on and patiently waiting her turn. So, we put our hands on her and said, "Jody, God made you and, well, you know, that's about it." I'm glad she didn't understand, because it's only humans who are made in the image and likeness of God, and only humans can become saints. Even though this exercise made me a bit uncomfortable, it was a tangible way of showing love ... even to Jody.

Our God is a merciful and loving God of reconciliation. When he forgives you, he means it. When you seek his forgiveness in the Sacrament of Reconciliation, he forgives you, and he means it. When he calls us to the Eucharistic table, he is calling us as his children to our baptismal promises and to partake in the salvation he offers, and he means it.

You might still have a knot that you're working on, but you need to have every confidence that because you are a child of God he wants to remove that knot from your life so that you can be the saint and disciple he yearns for you to be.

Don't you dare look in the mirror and say, "I'm no good," because God says, "You are my child, and you were made in my image and likeness."

Never underestimate the power behind those words. We don't often hear positive affirmations in today's world. We are told we are too fat or too thin or too tall or too short or not smart enough or too smart, but God says, "You're perfect just the way I made you."

You were made in the image and likeness of God. That's your true identity. Never forget it.

Chapter Eight

The Gift of Gifts

"Find something you're passionate about
and keep tremendously interested in it."
— Julia Child

THE SUMMER BEFORE Jennifer and I were married, I got it in my head that when we moved into our apartment I wanted it to be a cool, artsy place. I had never painted before, although I had done cartooning, but I went out, bought a bunch of canvases and tubes of paint, and was determined to figure out how to mesh it all into something worthwhile.

For months I painted up a storm, connecting deeply with something that apparently had been just waiting to explode out of me. We had paintings all over the walls in our little one-bedroom apartment. A couple years later, Jennifer got pregnant; thinking that paint and turpentine were probably not good to leave in the open around an infant, I put painting, indefinitely, on hold.

After years of suppressing various creative endeavors, and once our oldest was in high school, Jennifer surprised me and bought acrylics, new canvases, and new brushes and said, "I think it's time for you to start painting again." When I picked up the brushes, it was like something in me roared back to life, ravenous, as if suppressed for far too long.

What are the things that you wish that you had more time to do just for yourself? Do you want to paint? Do you want to play guitar? Do you want to read more? Do you want to write more? Do you just want to pray more?

If you could free up time each day, what would you do with it? If I gave you an extra two hours this week, how would you put them to good use? What would you do for you, to feed the soul and identity that God gave you?

I want you to think for a moment, because, again, this is important. Look back to when you were fifteen, sixteen, seventeen years old, or maybe even younger. What were the things you did when you were alone, that you did out of pure enjoyment? Did you draw? Did you play piano? Did you play guitar? Did you do science experiments just for fun? Did you act? What did you do? Did you dance? Did you sew? Did you play sports?

Now, for a moment, think about how you felt when you did those things. Try to reconnect with those feelings. The happiness. The joy.

What did those activities do for you?

I'll bet you felt alive, excited, even when you might have had to go to school and do other things. Even if you were busy, when you carved out the time to nurture yourself, these things brought you a certain level of being content, of being untied from the knots of life.

Now, let me ask you, do you still do those things today? Did they fade away at some point? Did they go away because you got busy?

Understanding that you are called to be a disciple, made in the image and likeness of God, that also means God has shared a part of himself with you in your personalities and interests.

And I want to stress this again: When we are in alignment with God and living as he desires us to live, we have greater peace and the knots of life begin to come undone.

But, although we know we are called to be disciples, sometimes we don't know quite how to do it. How do we actually take this identity that God has given us as his children and put it to work? On any given day you are going to have to deal with several different identities. You will go to work and have your work identity, and then at home you'll have your home identity, and then when you go out with friends you have another identity. But at the center of it all there's also an identity that is made up of your personal likes and dislikes, your interests and ambitions.

It's important to be aware and nurture in our lives these three factors: (1) what we need to do, (2) what we want to do, and (3) what we're created to do. We need to be aware and understand how they interconnect, overlap, and feed one another.

The need to do is easy and obvious: You need to do your job, you need to go to work, you need to take care of your family. What we want to do is worth considering. What we were created to do — discipleship, working toward sainthood — is more challenging, and we're going to get into that later.

So, let's look at how these fit together, starting with needs.

Besides work, there are some other needs as well. I mentioned earlier that I believe I need to write. When I gave it up for many years, I may not have realized it, but I was very disconcerted as I fell into nothing more than daily routines, because there was something that God put in me that I intentionally suppressed. This was a vital part of my personal identity. I need to undertake other creative endeavors as well, because these are things that God put into me. These interests that I have, they come from God. They are part of the identity he had in store for me when I was created, and I owe it both to God and myself to nurture these areas of my life.

He gives *you* the same kinds of things that may be solely unique to you and your life. These are things that feed your very soul on a daily basis. Prayer should be one of these things, but there are other things in our lives, too. Maybe you like to sew, or like to garden, or like to piddle around the garage, or build stuff. Too often, people relegate these things to the category of "goofing off," as if they were unimportant. But these are truly gifts, no matter how insignificant or silly someone else may find them, because God put those interests into you.

I think about my father, now in his eighties. He worked his tail off for many years, often never really allowing himself the time to have a hobby. Now that he's older, he spends hours in his garage, meticulously turning discarded chunks of wood on a lathe. He covers everything in sawdust until gorgeous wooden bowls emerge from the mess, genuine works of art. I just wonder how much happier he would have been in those forty or fifty years of working had he fed that part of himself — that is, if he had allowed that part of himself to come out and be fed?

If you like to write or draw, if you like to garden, if you like to tinker in your garage or rebuild engines — whatever it is — God has placed that in you. He has given us a certain sense in our souls that when we feed it we are acting in cooperation with God. In all these cases, we are creating with the Creator himself. He is allowing us to experience a little bit of his creativity, and that is part of our identity.

Our problem is that as spouses, as parents, as employees, we get caught up in the "important" things. Your marriage is vital. Your job is necessary. Your children are precious. But when we focus on these things to the exclusion of all else, we sometimes lose sight of what makes us who we are. When we allow ourselves to explore things we enjoy, to engage in creating with the Creator, then God can help us find ourselves again. We can find strength through these explorations, making us more successful in our relationships, occupations, and other areas of our lives. And, often, that happens in pretty amazing ways.

MAKING ROSARIES OUT OF KNOTS

In July 2002, I walked into the confessional where a priest waited for the next penitent while praying with a single-decade knotted rosary. I remember looking at the knots in his hand and thinking, "That's kind of cool."

I then made my confession and didn't think about that rosary again until a few months later. I was in a job at that time that I wasn't particularly happy with, and I was praying constantly for solace and direction. I was seeking God and just trying to figure out, "Why am I so unhappy?"

Then, for no reason whatsoever, one day as I sat in my crowded little cubicle, I remembered that priest's rosary. In the mere blip of a second I decided: "You know what? I'm going to figure out how to make one of those things." I went online and looked everywhere for some instructions, but couldn't find what I was looking for, especially instructions with pictures. Eventually, I found some basic text instructions and committed to giving it a try.

Now, when people look at me, a six-foot-five bald dude, they probably don't think of someone overly interested in macramélike arts. By no means am I the poster child for Hobby Lobby and Michael's, and they are probably not going to be hiring me anytime soon. Nevertheless, after work that day, I hit every craft store in town on a quest for twine. I was going to make one of these rosaries. Unable to find the No. 36 nylon twine described in the instructions, I instead landed this terribly ugly macramé cord, began messing with it, tying it in knots, trying my best to follow the instructions I found. I told myself, "Okay, it says go around my finger three times, pull it through," and I'd do it and the knot would disappear.

I kept trying and trying until, finally, I figured it out, and I was able to make one, single, pathetic knot. Then I made another, and another, and another, until, finally, I had completed the most hideous rosary ever seen. But I did it.

For the next few weeks it seemed like all I did was make rosaries. We went on vacation the week after I started making them, and I was walking down the beach, not looking at the ocean or glorious sunsets, but making rosaries with the twine dangling in the wind behind me.

That was the beginning of an apostolate called Rosary Army, which is dedicated to making, praying, and giving away all-twine knotted rosaries and encouraging others to do the same. The month after I made that first rosary, Pope John Paul II declared the Year of the Rosary and introduced the world to the Luminous Mysteries. Less than a year later, Rosary Army was incorporated as a nonprofit organization. Since then, either directly or indirectly, Rosary Army has been responsible for the distribution of millions of rosaries around the world, all because I got so addicted to doing something as silly as making knotted rosaries.

You see, that's how God works. He put in me the need to do something creative. That's a need. Then I had the want, the desire to learn how to make rosaries. And what happened next? Well, these all came together in what God made me to be — a disciple.

Let me put it this way: If you are called to be a disciple, if you are called to be a witness in this world, it can start with you saying yes to the smallest little initiative, the tiniest push from the Holy Spirit. I was actually feeding my soul, doing something I wanted to do when I made those first rosaries.

A few years after starting Rosary Army, Jennifer and I dove headfirst into podcasting, becoming the first Catholic apostolate ever to use podcasting technologies. From podcasting we helped start another Catholic apostolate that helped bring other people together creating Catholic media. Shortly after that, we were hired by Sirius XM to host a radio show. We did that for several years and eventually ended up in Denver, where I worked for the archdiocese as the executive director of the Office of Evangelization and Family Life Ministries.

Recently, God led us to Indiana, where I became the editorial director for a major Catholic publishing house. It all started with my asking myself the simple questions: What do I want to do? What is God calling me to do? So, don't tell me that God can't take something as simple as a piece of twine and make you into his disciple, because he can!

What about you? Are you willing to accept the identity — the skills and desires and interests — that God has given you? Are you willing to accept that you are made in the image and likeness of God? Are you willing to take steps to see if maybe God is taking you someplace amazing to bless other people in this world as his disciple?

What do you need to do?

What do you want to do?

What were you made for?

By now, your mind might be a swirl of activity, as ideas are rushing to the surface. For some, this might cause additional knots of anxiety. But, in our search for identity, as we're seeking God and how God has touched us all individually, I think it's worthwhile to write things down. I'm a list person. I always have index cards in my pocket for making lists and writing stuff down. If you're not doing that already, I recommend that you start writing down what you think you *want* to do in your life. Notice, I said, "want to do."

The things you are responsible for — such as your commitment to being a Cub Scout pack leader or doing your job — are probably "need to do" items, so you don't need to write those down. Just start making a list of what you want to do. Maybe it's an old passion like my painting or my dad's turning bowls on a lathe. Maybe it's something from your youth, or something brand new that you want to explore. Maybe you're thinking: "You know what? I always wanted to explore that underwater basket-weaving class. Maybe now's the time; maybe it's time to find a new hobby." Write it down. And once you've written these things down, as you continue searching take these ideas to prayer.

Some people may find this exercise difficult, especially if you are not used to thinking about what you *want* to do. But out of the struggle will come some semblance of your true self, your true identity. So, if you are struggling as you seek to find and accept your true identity, I encourage you right now to say this prayer:

Lord God, I thank you for my difficulties. I thank you for the knots in my life, as painful as they might be. I thank you for my struggles. I thank you for my inadequacies. I thank you for all of the ways, Lord, that you're constantly pulling me to you. Lord God, I come to you now with thanksgiving, I ask you to free me from my anxieties, to help me to completely surrender myself to you. With thanksgiving I offer myself to you right now. Please rejuvenate me. Please help me start working to be the dis-

ciple, the saint, that you call me to be. Lord, I
ask you to live up to the promise you made, that
when I make my requests known to you with
thanksgiving you will allow me to experience
the peace of God, which passes all understanding. I ask that you keep my mind focused on
Christ Jesus. Amen.

Chapter Nine

An Examination of Knots

"When we do not listen to [God], when we do not follow his will, we do concrete things that demonstrate our lack of trust in him — for that is what sin is — and a kind of knot is created deep within us."
— Pope Francis

WE'VE TALKED ABOUT our core identity and things in our busy lives that create stress and knots. But another knot that we have control over is the acknowledgement of our sinfulness and the need for a savior to forgive us, as well as our need to recommit daily to turning away from sin.

Sin, quite simply, makes us stupid. We are all sinners, and sometimes we allow ourselves to fall into pervasive and recurring sins. Or, worse, we fall so deeply into sin that we trick ourselves into believing our sins are excusable, and even allowable.

The truth is that when we are in a state of sin, whether it's everyday venial sins or, worse, mortal sin, we have a knot that we carry all the time.

Sin can make us feel separated from those we love. It can cause depression, loneliness, fear, and anger. It can lead us so far from ourselves that we sometimes think we can never get back. When we are living in sin, doing things we know we shouldn't be doing, it weighs us down. Sometimes they can be big things — like having an affair, and all the lies and deception that go with such a big sin (don't worry, Jennifer, that's just an example). But it can be a smaller sin, too, such as neglecting to say regular prayers or being short-tempered with our kids.

When we are in a state of sin, big or small, it's a steady, ongoing drag on our lives and a constant source of knots. Remember when I said that sometimes knots can be blessings down the road? Well, the knots that are created by sin can become a blessing when they force us to take action and change our lives for the better.

The first step on the path of being untied from the knots of sin is a practice called an examination of conscience. We have to look with honesty and courage at what we have done, not only to identify recent sins but to see more clearly the knots created by those sins.

The *Catechism of the Catholic Church* tells us:

> The education of the conscience is a lifelong task. From the earliest years, it awakens the child to the knowledge and practice of the interior law recognized by conscience. Prudent education teaches virtue; it prevents or cures fear, selfishness and pride, resentment arising from

guilt, and feelings of complacency, born of human weakness and faults. The education of the conscience guarantees freedom and engenders peace of heart. (1784)

We should make an examination of conscience a regular practice, not only to help us confess our sins, but to summon up genuine sorrow — contrition — for what we have done.

Let's look at some of the more common sources of sin in our modern-day lives. I encourage you to take these items to prayer, to ask the Holy Spirit to move your heart if any of these items resonate with you, and maybe even keep a list that will assist you during your next confession.

Again, think not only from the perspective of sins committed recently, but ask yourself if you've been holding a grudge against yourself for any sins from your past.

Many people have knots from sexual sin. Maybe you're feeling tied up in knots because of your past or current use of contraception. Or maybe you have had an abortion in the past. Or maybe you had sex before marriage or with someone who is not your spouse. Have you thought lustfully about other people or masturbated?

But there are other, often less obvious, things that might be holding us back. Maybe you have hurt someone with your words. Sometimes our words can really damage people even more than our actions. They can almost kill a part of a person. The words that we say to others can have a long-term damaging effect. Perhaps we have said things to other people that have caused them to feel a little less of a person. Maybe you've said something in the past and you still regret it. Well, that's important to remember and confess.

What if someone has said something to you and you have not forgiven that person? Are you holding on to a grudge? Have you given in to envy? Envy is not simply being jealous of something that someone has, it's wishing that they didn't have it, or wishing them harm because they do have it. In other words, it's wishing that someone else didn't have the blessings they enjoy.

What about using things such as astrology, horoscopes, or fortune-telling? I have confessed about even looking at the simple, silly little horoscopes that are in the newspapers around the comics pages. I would confess it because in the back of my mind I knew I was thinking maybe there's a little truth there. Maybe you've done the same thing.

Have you sinned against your faith by seriously believing in New Age or Scientology, or by engaging in the occult? These are all things that not only can take hold in our lives but can haunt us for years. When I was seventeen years old, I was baby-sitting some kids whose parents had actually given them a Ouija board for Christmas. So, one night, they show me this Ouija board, and we start messing with it. I had no idea of just how dangerous it is to play with stuff like this. I asked the board, "How old will I be when I die?" For the next several decades I was haunted by the fact that this Ouija board moved to a four and then it moved to a two. This stupid board told me that I would die when I was forty-two years old. From then until my forty-third birthday I had told only one other person about this — a priest, when I went to confession. I confessed that sin, yet allowed it to weigh on me for all those years. It was something that would boil to the surface and manifest itself in irrational worry. It was a terrible, stupid burden. Think about how ridiculous it is to have been worried about something like that for years, but it had opened up the doors to the occult. There's a reason why Scripture and the Catechism teach clearly against these things — because we're opening the door for the devil, who uses things such as this to make us think we don't need God's guidance for the future, that we can discover the future for ourselves.

To this point, let's be honest and acknowledge that evil spirits exist in this world. They want to mess with us and keep us tied in knots. Evil spirits want to keep us from experiencing peace in our lives. Evil spirits of discouragement, anger, envy, and sloth do not want you to experience the freedom that comes with following the will of Jesus Christ. A lot of times we open doors to evil spirits in our lives, and they try to take residence. That's why we need to forgive ourselves in the name of Jesus Christ. Evil spirits cannot stand the name of Jesus

Christ. Furthermore, we can renounce these things. We can say: "In the name of Jesus Christ, I renounce any use of anything that has to do with the occult [or sexual sins, or any other sin]. In the name of Jesus Christ, I rebuke any evil spirits that may exist in my life."

There might be other things weighing us down. Have we allowed ourselves to be bound by taking the name of God in vain? Have we committed sacrilege by showing disrespect to holy objects? Have we remembered to keep holy the Sabbath? Have we skipped Mass on Sundays and holy days of obligation? Do we show disrespect by leaving Mass early? Have we set a bad example for our children by casually missing Mass? By not paying attention or joining in prayers? Do we give of our time and talent? Have we been selfish in the way we support the Church? Do we work unnecessarily on Sundays? What about honoring mother and father? Do we make sure that our children are being educated in the faith?

Have you committed an act of violence or abuse, whether physical, sexual, emotional, or in other ways?

It amazes me how many people walk around carrying the weight of their sin when they don't have to. So, let me get this basic advice out of the way: If you've done something you know was wrong listed above, or maybe something else not on the list but which follows you every day like an unshakable shadow, and if you genuinely feel bad about it, simply go to confession. Just do it. Be contrite and seek God's forgiveness and mercy that knows no boundaries. You'll feel better. It's as simple as that. That advice alone should be worth the price of this book.

Even still, though the solution to the knots of sin is really that simple, we don't always want it, often because the idea of confessing can be scary.

"YOUR SINS ARE FORGIVEN"

The Sacrament of Reconciliation is a healing sacrament. Our sins open a chasm between us and God, and confession heals that rift. If you sin and are contrite, and you seek reconciliation, God does forgive you. You are forgiven. You are healed.

But, unfortunately, that doesn't always mean "case closed" for us. It can be a little more complex than that.

What if you've sought God's forgiveness, but the weight of sin still seems to be pulling you down? What if you don't seem able to break through and stop doing the things you know you shouldn't be doing, kind of like when you can't not eat that next potato chip. You just can't stop.

How many times have you gone to confession and then walked out knowing that you still might commit that same sin? There are times in confession when I'm praying the Act of Contrition and saying the words that I resolve not to sin again and already thinking, "This ain't going to last long."

That is another knot, another source of stress. I recommend this quote from Saint Paul's Letter to the Romans: "Since all have sinned and fall short of the glory of God, they are justified by his grace as a gift, through the redemption which is in Christ Jesus" (3:23–24).

We know that we have been justified by the gift of redemption, which is in Christ Jesus, but do we live as such? When we don't place our trust in Jesus, we are destined to have an ongoing knot in our lives. If you find yourself in this situation, I encourage you to remember St. Paul's words that we have all fallen short but are justified through Christ. No matter what habit you're struggling to break, I urge you to regularly seek the mercy of Christ through the Sacrament of Reconciliation.

But there is something else to consider. I can count on one hand the times where I felt God speak to me so clearly that it was undeniable that it was God. I don't hear: "Greg, hello, this is God. Good morning. Here's your agenda for today." Most of the time, my prayer consists of sitting in a chair repeatedly asking: "Are you there? Hello? Are you there? Hello? Can you help me out here, God? Hello? Can you help me hear you?"

But one time, so clearly and undeniably, I actually heard God. I used to work close to a nearby church that had Mass every day at noon. I would go to Mass Monday through Thursday, but on Friday the church offered Adoration after Mass. So, on Friday I went to Adoration instead of Mass. One Friday, I had the opportunity to go to confession before Adoration.

As usual, I walked into the confessional, bared my soul, and walked out knowing I was forgiven. But like so many times before, the weight was still there. Regret remained — humiliation, anguish, and embarrassment for things I'd done years before, things that after countless confessions continued to follow me wherever I went, no matter how good I tried to be.

So, that particular Friday, after I walked out of the confessional, I took a seat in the pew in front of the monstrance. I *knew* I just went to confession, I *knew* I was forgiven, but I still felt so weighed down, not necessarily by what I just confessed, but really by things that I did in my past, as far back as college and high school and even before.

I was stupid when I was younger. I did stupid things in my youth, things that I wish I hadn't done, things that followed me for many years. And I just couldn't stop thinking about these things — the bad decisions, the bad priorities, the sins in which I'd willingly engaged.

So, I asked God, "Why do I still feel so weighed down with this burden, of these things from so long ago?" Then I heard in my heart our loving and merciful Savior say: "Not only have I forgiven your sins, but I already carried the cross of your sins as well. I carried the heavy burden of your sins as well."

This struck me like a bolt of lightning at the time and continues to impact me to this day. I have to remind myself regularly that, yes, we will have crosses that we will have to carry, difficulties in life, challenges, and heavy burdens. But the crosses of our sins are not burdens we must continue to carry once we've given them to God and sought his forgiveness in confession.

Let me say this clearly to you: We do not have to carry the crosses of our sins anymore. You do not have to carry the crosses of your past sins anymore.

Jesus Christ, in the Garden of Gethsemane, took the weight of the world's sins on his shoulders. He carried the cross of our sins, and as the sacrificial Lamb of God and Savior of the World, he died on the cross for our sins. He carried that bigger cross so that we would not have to.

And oftentimes forgiveness of self and forgiveness of others is one of our bigger crosses and one of the tightest knots that must be untied. It was absolutely life-changing for me when I realized that I not only needed to forgive myself, but I needed to allow Jesus to carry the cross he already promised to carry for me.

Through the years, there were also other people in my life, besides myself, that I needed to forgive. I might have said I forgave them and would pray for them, but the feeling of unforgiveness would linger. There have been a few people in my life who were the No. 1 topic of confession for many years, in my thoughts and in my words. But if I was to accept the forgiveness of Christ, and to allow him to carry the burden of my sins, I also had to learn how to forgive others as Christ forgives me.

Do you ever have those imaginary conversations when you're driving down the road by yourself, shouting down someone who isn't even there? "I'll tell you another thing. The next time I see you, I'm going to tell you this, and I'm going to tell you another thing.

And don't you tell me that I told you that." I did that for several years after a trusted coworker hurt me. We both ended up saying damaging things to the other, and while I thought I had forgiven him, I actually was having trouble forgiving myself. It took a long time, and a very public falling out, before we actually got to the place where real forgiveness was possible. All that time I was carrying around the knot of lack of forgiveness, for both him and me. And it wasn't until we really forgave each other in Jesus' name that the knot finally untied.

That's why it's so important that we offer each other — and even ourselves — verbal apologies and verbal forgiveness. Not long ago I was drawn to ask my son Walter to forgive me for any of the ways I might have failed him as he was growing up. I told him if there were any things he was holding on to, to please tell me and I would ask his forgiveness. We talked about several things, and I hope that he knows that if I ever fail him in the future, I will always be willing to ask his forgiveness in the name of Jesus.

Sometimes we try to forgive and be forgiven through our own strength, our own volition, rather than praying and forgiving in the name of Jesus Christ.

Is there someone — maybe yourself — whom you've struggled to forgive? If so, I want you to stop right now and pray this prayer: "In the name of Jesus Christ, I forgive _____ for _____." If you've struggled to forgive yourself for actions of your past, say, "In the name of Jesus Christ, I forgive myself for _____."

Forgiveness on our own is powerful, but forgiveness in the name of Jesus Christ is *redeeming*. When I stopped trying to carry the weight of my own sins and said, "In the name of Jesus Christ, I forgive myself for my actions of the past. In the name of Jesus Christ, I forgive that person who hurt me," I felt an overwhelming sense of relief. Jesus Christ, who carried the weight of our sins, can help us in his name to forgive others and to forgive ourselves.

I'm going to give you an exercise. You don't necessarily have to write it down on a piece of paper, but I think that it's helpful to have it in black and white, where you can look at it. What I want you to do is make a list of people you need to forgive in Jesus' name, starting with yourself. When I did this, it filled two sides of a notecard, and, believe me, I write very small. As you do this, you might want to pray: "Who do I need to forgive in the name of Jesus? Holy Spirit, give me the names of the people I need to forgive, starting with myself." Write down every single name that comes to mind.

Next, I want you to take each of these names to Jesus in prayer and forgive them. Be sure to include yourself on the list. Pray: "In the name of Jesus Christ I forgive myself. In the name of Jesus Christ, I forgive _____." You might have to go over the list more than once, but when you know you have truly forgiven that person, cross his or her name off the list. When you've forgiven everyone, tear up the list and throw it away, because now it belongs to Jesus, not you. Let him carry that cross.

I can't stress this enough: If you want to experience true forgiveness, and if you want to give true forgiveness, it must be in the name of Jesus Christ. One of the first and most critical steps in having knots untied in your life is forgiving ourselves and others in Jesus' name. After that forgiveness prayer, be thankful for whatever circumstances might have led to those bad things.

Removing the knots that keep you from God can be a difficult thing. Forgiveness is the place to begin, but if we are to make sure the knots don't come back, we need to develop a strong prayer life. As I've been asking throughout this book, what are the areas of your life that have you tied up in knots? Now, I'll ask the question: If you could have those knots untied, what could you do for yourself? What could you do for your family? What could you do for this world?

Chances are, those knots keep you from being the disciple you were called to be. Your knots are trying to tell you: "You have to carry this cross around, this cross of your sin. You're not good enough."

Don't believe it.

If you didn't have to carry those knots around anymore, what could you do instead? Could you paint a picture? Could you write a book? Could you lead a class at church? Could you talk more confidently to your friends and family about Jesus Christ? Could you have more loving relationships?

I want you to think about you changing the world. I want you to think about the fact that you are a disciple. You were called to do this. You were called to have a ribbon of life — with all knots untied — that's smooth and malleable, and that allows you to be free to serve so that you can be the disciple that God wants you to be.

What is Jesus wanting you to do? What is Jesus telling you to do? Seek him. Seek his mother. Seek the guidance of his Holy Spirit. Seek forgiveness. And trust that the knots of your life can and will be undone.

Chapter Ten

Prayer and Other Tools

*"Among Violet's many useful skills was a vast
knowledge of different types of knots."*
— Lemony Snicket,
A Series of Unfortunate Events

MY OLDER BROTHERS were trying to convince me to
walk off a cliff.

Literally.

It was just a couple weeks before I graduated high
school, and Paul and Scott persuaded me to join them
on a last-minute excursion to Kentucky's Red River
Gorge state park. Somehow, I'd managed to follow them
up the steep ninety-degree incline of a slate rock wall.
Climbing up was easy and exciting, but when I reached
the summit and unsteadily peeked over the edge of the
wall I'd just ascended, my head spun with vertigo at the
ground now two hundred feet below me.

"Now's the fun part," Scott said, as he pulled up
the rope he'd harnessed into carabiners as we climbed.
"Now we rappel down."

Stupidly trusting my sibling, I straddled into an awkward harness onto which Scott latched another metal carabiner before looping a length of rope through it.

"I'll hold it from this end and you descend backwards."

I looked over the edge again, trying to piece together how this would work. I lowered myself to my hands and knees and began to crawl toward the cliff's ledge.

"What are you doing?" Paul asked.

"I'm going to start climbing down," I answered.

"No, you just walk backwards," Scott said.

"What?"

"Off the cliff."

"What?" I asked again.

"Just stand up and walk backwards off the edge and I'll belay the rope as you go down."

"You're insane," I scoffed.

"It's perfectly safe," Scott assured me. This was the same guy who once convinced a kid we knew that a jock strap was a Batman mask.

"You just walk backwards down the cliff," Paul said.

"Walk," I said. "Backwards. Down the cliff."

"Right," my brothers confirmed.

"You realize that makes no sense," I told them.

In the minutes that followed I devolved into a sobbing mess, terrified and untrusting. What would the other end of the rope be tied to? How would I know the rope wouldn't come untied? How would I possibly walk backwards off the side of what now felt like Mount Everest without crashing to my death?

At some point, realizing I'd either die in the fall or die from starvation after my brothers inevitably abandoned me on the top of that rock, I closed my eyes, one hand perilously gripping a strand of rope that ran through the carabiner while the other end draped like a dangling snake toward the ground below me.

And I stepped backwards.

And the rope held.

And I didn't go crashing to the ground.

And after joyfully making it back to our base at the bottom of the rock, fear was suddenly replaced with the realization that I was somehow energized by the entire experience, more aware and confident than I'd ever been before, nearly drunk with the endorphins of having not only gone outside of my comfort zone, but having blasted it to smithereens.

Granted, that exuberance was due in part to being only seventeen at the time, but even still, I can't help looking back on that day in the woods and seeing several critical components that have become benchmarks throughout my life:

- Learning to trust people who'd experienced similar difficulties
- Allowing myself to experience new and sometimes frightening situations
- Discovering within myself the ability to do more than I would have believed

- Reliance on having the right tools at the right time, and then using them
- The importance of having an anchor on which to tether myself in the midst of difficulties

It's natural to think of knots as gnarled and tangled messes that should be immediately untied. But in the case of my initiation into the world of rock climbing, a knot was my best friend that day, literally lowering me to safety. While a knot can bind us up inside, a knot can also be a point of strength that holds things together.

Looking at the most stressful times in my life, times when I most needed to understand that God was holding the rope that was keeping me from crashing to the ground, it was the particularly stressful moments that often brought me back into a stronger practice of deeper prayer.

Taking time to seek nourishment for our souls, nourishment for our journey through this life, is an absolute necessity that lies at the heart of all we do. This nourishment, of course, is found through the development and practice of an ongoing prayer life and through actively seeking a deeper relationship with God our Father; Jesus Christ, our brother, savior, and king; and with the Holy Spirit, our Paraclete and source of strength and guidance in this life.

Our prayer life and a deepening of our relationship with the Holy Trinity must be more than simply begging God for help in times of need, or showing up for Mass on Sundays (which you're obligated to do anyway). We are nourished through the daily practice of seeking God and spending time getting to know him through silent prayer, through reading Scripture, through studying great books and the words of those who have journeyed before and alongside us.

It is often incredibly difficult for us to figure out how to obtain this spiritual nourishment. It's hard to develop routine and virtue and positive habits — just as it's difficult to count calories or exercise daily — but we know it's something we need to do, and it's infinitely rewarding when we're able to do so.

Excuses are easy to come up with when thinking about developing a solid prayer life, but Ecclesiastes 11:4 reminds us, "If you wait until the wind and the weather are just right, you will never plant anything and never harvest anything" (Good News Translation). So, I'd like to suggest some prayer ideas to hopefully re-energize your prayer life.

A great way to pray is the practice of *lectio divina*, or divine reading: the practice of reading Scripture not as a text but as the living word of God. Traditionally, *lectio divina* has four parts, or steps: reading, meditation, prayer, and contemplation. First, read a passage of Scripture. Next, meditate on it by entering into the passage. For example, if you read about the wedding feast at Cana, which I told you was one of my favorite stories, you might place yourself as one of the servants filling the water jars. You ponder the words, allowing the Holy Spirit to inspire you as to their meaning in your life. Third, pray whatever comes from your heart. And, finally, contemplate the passage as the Word of God, putting Jesus at the center and "resting" in the text. In *lectio divina*, you don't analyze the words. You let them penetrate into your soul and allow God to speak to you.

There are so many wonderful Bible-study books to assist you in the process of reading the Word of God. *Bringing the Gospel to Life* series by George Martin and *Walking with God* by Jeff Cavins and Tim Gray are wonderful books to accompany you through Scripture.

Then there is the Rosary. The Rosary is, at its heart, the prayer of the Gospel. Starting with the Joyful Mysteries, then the Luminous, the Sorrowful, and, finally, the Glorious, it celebrates the entire story of Christ's salvation, from the announcement of his birth through his kingship in heaven. When you meditate on the mysteries of the Rosary, you are meditating on the work of salvation. And you can even use the Bible to enhance this prayer, focusing on the events of the life of Christ. Plus, you are doing it in union with Mary. What could be better? As I mentioned earlier, my family even runs an apostolate dedicated to giving away a rosary to whoever needs one. If you contact us at rosaryarmy.com, we will send you a free all-twine knotted rosary.

Novenas can also be powerful prayers, seeking God's help in specific situations and challenges. In case you're not familiar with a novena, it's saying a set of prayers or a particular prayer for nine days in a row while focusing on a specific intention. There are novenas asking for the intercession of Mary, Saint Joseph, Saint John Paul II, and just about every saint you can imagine. If asking for the intercession of saints is something you struggle with, then keep in mind that it's no different than if you were to ask me to pray for you (and please know that I do). Do you think my prayer for you will reach the loving heart of God? Then you can trust even more that he hears and answers the prayers of people much closer to him than I am, who are already in heaven with him.

You can pray a novena to any saint for any reason — all it takes is nine days of petition and prayer, usually accompanied by a Rosary. If you do pray to a saint, normally the novena ends on their feast day, so count back nine days to know when to start. But you can pray a novena anytime!

Years ago I prayed my very first fifty-four-day novena. That means I prayed six, nine-day Rosary novenas in a row. I prayed the Rosary every single day for fifty-four days for a very specific intention. As part of this devotion, the first three novenas — the first twenty-seven days — you pray in petition. Then, the second set of three novenas — the next twenty-seven days — you pray in thanksgiving, even if your prayer has not yet been answered. You offer up that thanksgiving to Jesus Christ immediately. At the end of my fifty-four days, my prayer was not answered, but I had incredible peace, and I had a great amount of trust that it would be answered.

Another great way to pray is by praying over your children. Sure, we pray for our kids, but praying over them is different. When you pray over your children, you are not just praying for their needs, rather you are literally covering them in prayer, just as Aaron the high priest and brother of Moses did:

"The LORD said to Moses, 'Say to Aaron and his sons, Thus you shall bless the sons of Israel: you shall say to them,

"The LORD bless you and keep you: / The LORD make his face to shine upon you, and be gracious to you: / The LORD lift up his countenance upon you, and give you peace.

"So shall they put my name upon the sons of Israel, and I will bless them'" (Nm 6:22–27).

I've prayed this prayer over my children since they were born, and, God willing, I will someday pray it over my grandchildren.

One of the most effective things to do as a family is Total Consecration. What is that? Total Consecration to Jesus through Mary is an absolutely beautiful exercise to increase your spirituality and ability to truly serve our Lord Jesus Christ. The basic premise was set forth by Saint Louis-Marie Grignion de Montfort, who said that Jesus came into the world through Mary, and for us to always be assured of being close to Jesus we should go through Mary. Initially, this idea may seem strange. I will admit I was completely confused when someone first proposed it to me years ago. Why consecration?

And why consecration through Mary? What does that even mean?

Consecration means to set aside for a sacred purpose. Mary's life was set aside for the sole purpose of serving Our Lord. By following her example, we, too, can completely give ourselves to Christ in a fundamental way that consecrates us to him. We give our lives to him in service and love. We consecrate ourselves in order to be more devoted to the Lord and his Blessed Mother. It helps us grow in holiness and increases our faith, hope, and love. It is a prayerful and focused method of drawing closer to Jesus. My wife and I attribute Total Consecration as *really* putting ourselves to work for Jesus. All of the major initiatives and responsibilities God has given us followed consecrating ourselves.

Consecration consists of a thirty-three-day period of prayerful preparation followed by the act of consecration itself. This preparation includes a preliminary period of twelve days, during which we endeavor "to free ourselves from the spirit of the world." This initial twelve days is followed by a second period of three weeks. The first of these three weeks is devoted to the knowledge of ourselves, the second to that of the Blessed Virgin, and the third to that of Jesus Christ. The object of this consecration is to cast off the spirit of the world, which is contrary to that of Jesus Christ, in order to acquire fully the spirit of Jesus Christ through the Blessed Virgin.

The cycle of preparation (the prayers and meditations take approximately ten to fifteen minutes per day) typically begins thirty-three days before a Marian feast day, which allows the consecration to take place on that feast. You can find the prayers and meditations at http://totalconsecration.com.

Another great way to surround yourself with prayer is to enthrone your home to the Sacred Heart of Jesus. Jesus promised Saint Margaret Mary Alacoque that he "will bless the home in which the image of my Sacred Heart shall be exposed and honored." When we display (enthrone) a picture of the Sacred Heart and ask Jesus to be the king of our home, we have an outward sign of our inward trust and adoration of the Lord. We make our very homes a shrine to Jesus and his mother. This was so important to our family that I even did a custom painting we hung in our home, had a priest over to lead our family through the enthronement, and really tried to make Jesus the center and focal point of our home.

Many other traditional prayers, such as the Chaplet of Divine Mercy and St. Michael's Prayer, can be found in the Appendix. I encourage you to take a look at them, to see if one or more touches your heart. If so, begin to pray that prayer on a regular basis. I can assure you that if you do, you will begin to find more peace in your life and gain a greater understanding of God's will for your life.

When our minds are a bustling thoroughfare of blaring thoughts and noise, it's nearly impossible to maintain peace. While throughout this book I touch on practical ways to find more peace, the ultimate solution to untying knots in your life will be a divinely proven method of prayer that I'll dive into with more detail soon.

But, as another starting point, even if your faith in God is somewhat lacking, I'm confident that there is the potential for great peace in just a few moments of silent meditation, of slowing your breath and picturing a loving God who loves you as his child and yearns to love you in a way that no one else can.

If you struggle with prayer, it's okay to start with just closing your eyes and being silent for a few minutes. But if you want more than that, below is an approachable four-step prayer method (and another acronym) that I recommend you try for a week, and observe whether you experience a greater level of peace and closeness with God. Even better, if you have the opportunity to stop in at your local parish and spend time in silence there, this prayer may lead you into an even greater bevy of spiritual riches.

RAPT IN PRAYER

This technique, which can last as long as you want or can be prayed in just a minute or two, is called RAPT, which stands for Repentance, Adoration, Petition, and Thanksgiving.

Repentance
Upon quieting yourself, start by acknowledging your own inadequacies, sins, and downright stupidity (and

we're *all* stupid from time to time). Using this method every day acts as a reminder for a daily examination of conscience (such as discussed in Chapter 9: "An Examination of Knots"). Ask yourself: "What have I done (or thought or failed to do) in the last twenty-four hours that may have offended God or someone else I love?" Recall all of these things, summon up true contrition and sorrow, and bring these things to God in prayer and ask for his forgiveness. Later, also bring these to the Sacrament of Reconciliation to receive the graces available there to strengthen you throughout your life.

Adoration
To adore God can be as simple as taking a moment to slow down and acknowledge his sovereignty as God the Father, creator of heaven and earth. Therefore, the next step is to think of God truly as your father and put yourself in his presence, approaching him as his beloved child. He cares about you. He loves you. He wants to hear from you. Now, acknowledge Jesus Christ, your brother and your king, who loves you so much he allowed himself to be put on the cross and killed for you. Think about your love for him or, if you don't yet have a relationship with Christ, perhaps consider what that would look like and invite him into your life at this moment. Last, think about the power of the Holy Spirit in your life, and how dependent you are on him, and the graces he wants to deliver into your soul through the sacraments.

Petition

Now that you've taken time to apologize and acknowledge God as the one in control of your life, share with him your most pressing needs and the desires of your heart. Ask for an outpouring of grace to live the kind of life God wants for you, as well as for the strength to carry whatever crosses may be in your life.

Thanksgiving

Consciously taking time to be thankful makes a huge difference in your relationship with God. But even beyond that, developing an attitude of thankfulness for the blessings in life is a simple antidote to pessimism. Just as with repenting, with this last step stop and think about all the ways in the past twenty-four hours that God has been there for you. Think of all the small ways (like getting you home without bad traffic or simply for a nice comfortable bed) or the big ways (such as good health reports or answers to past prayers). Try to think of every single good thing that God has done in your life since you last prayed this RAPT prayer.

Taking all of these steps together, here's an example of the prayer in action (which I invite you to stop and pray right now):

Dear Lord, [R-Repentance] I'm sorry for not taking more time to talk with you yesterday, for allowing the busyness of the day to take over, and for any times I may have sinned against you (at this point you may want to include specific times you were weak). [A-Adoration] You are God, my father, who made me and everything around me. You are Jesus Christ, my savior, who loved me so much you *died* for me. You are God the Holy Spirit, who inspires and directs me in my life. [P-Petition] I ask you to help me be a better person. I ask you to remove the knots in my life and help me to have more peace today. Please help me understand how best to be like Jesus. Please help the people in my life who are suffering. [T-Thanksgiving] I thank you for being my God, and I offer up my day — both the good and the bad — to you. I love you, Lord. Thank you for everything. Amen.

I hope you take on this challenge. I hope you find ways to pray that nourish your soul. I hope you take the time to start nurturing the identity that God has given you. I hope you take the time to start feeding that part of you God has placed in you that is unique to you and you alone. I hope you will start to live in that identity in truth and know with certainty that you are indeed made in the image and likeness of God.

But most of all, I hope for you the words of Philippians 4:6–7: "Have no anxiety about anything, but in everything by prayer and supplication with thanksgiving let your requests be made known to God. And the peace of God, which passes all understanding, will keep your hearts and your minds in Christ Jesus."

Mary, Undoer of Knots, pray for us.

Chapter Eleven

The Ultimate Untier of Knots

"The knot of Eve's disobedience was loosed
by the obedience of Mary."
— Saint Irenaeus

So far in this book I have talked about steps we can take to recognize, accept, and begin to untie the many knots in our lives. As you begin this chapter, I encourage you to open yourself to allow God to get to work, not only on the knots you think need to be untied, but even on knots you're not aware of. These could be knots from your past or knots you're dealing with now without realizing it. While we have to do everything we can to untie our knots, inevitably there will be knots in our lives that we can't see, many completely beyond our control.

This doesn't mean we should just give up on finding peace — far from it. But it does require a whole new level of trust on our part.

Ultimately, it's important to reflect on what we're seeking: Is it an exact answer to prayer in the way we think it has to be answered, or peace from God in the midst of whatever difficulty we're experiencing? If we have peace from God, it doesn't matter what we're struggling through.

I will also share some advice I was given from a priest long ago: the two wings of prayer are fasting and almsgiving. If you're already praying, great. But also seek ways to be more generous with others, whether financially or with your time and talents. The Lord may occasionally give you the grace to fast from food. But if your prayers need an extra push, you could fast in other ways as well. Give up television, the Internet, or your smartphone for a day. Give up coffee for a day, or go without breakfast. Jesus said that certain demons couldn't be cast out without prayer and fasting. So, we know that some prayers require the added strength of fasting and almsgiving. If you're finding that your knot is not coming untied, maybe God is calling you to go deeper.

Now I'm going to lay out the simple game plan that has been a saving grace not only for me but for thousands of people for centuries. Many people who have utilized the following form of prayer have received grace and peace in the worst situations in life. Others have discovered simple solutions to problems both large and small.

I can even attest to taking on the following novena for a huge employment-related knot in my life and, within seventy-two hours of finishing these prayers, I not only got a lead on a new job, but Jesus untied a knot I didn't realize had tied me up for over thirty years.

The story began when I was a kid between fourth and seventh grades, when my family was a foster family for newborn infants. The youngest baby we got was just two days old, while others came to us a month or more after being born. They all had different backgrounds, different reasons for ending up with us. One baby's mom was in prison for check fraud, and some babies came to us with no stories at all. They just needed a home, so my parents took them in.

Everyone in my family latched onto different babies for different reasons. My brother Paul's favorite was a curly-haired little girl named Talitha. My sister Robbie had an affinity for a baby named Jerry (probably because that was her boyfriend — and now husband's — name).

My favorite was Sabrina, who came to us at just four days old. But she wasn't my favorite at first. In fact, for the first two months we had her, Sabrina would shake and scream uncontrollably. My mother was certain that Sabrina's birth mother must have been on drugs and had passed the addiction to Sabrina. But then, suddenly, she stopped crying; instead, she became full of smiles. One thing that was unique was that her smile drooped just a little on the right side. For the first seven months of her life, Sabrina was my sister, and my parents even brought up the idea of potentially adopting her. But then, as a new school year began, we got the call that she would be leaving us. A family had been identified to adopt her. And like that, Sabrina was gone. There was to be no contact between us and her new family. And that was that.

We moved to another state shortly thereafter, and life continued. But as the years plodded by, with every relocation or life change I'd find myself thinking about Sabrina. I wondered where she was, always regretting the fact that we had not adopted her. Twelve years later, I remember standing on the altar about to marry my wife and feeling regret that my sister Sabrina was not there. Each time we had another child over the ensuing years, I wished my little sister was still around.

Over three decades passed, and in early 2016 I found myself struggling with my career path. I felt somewhat derailed, most certainly tied in knots, as I sought God's direction in discerning next steps. In desperation, I started a nine-day novena to Mary, Undoer of Knots, seeking to be untied from the knots in my life that I thought revolved just around my work.

Two days after I finished that novena, I received a call asking if I had potential interest in a new job in a new state. Over the next day I marveled at the fact that Jesus, through his mother, had answered my prayer so rapidly. I had prayed this prayer in the past seemingly to no avail, but now, suddenly, there was hope and potential for the future.

But here's where the story gets interesting.

The next day, three days after completing that novena, I suddenly had the compulsion to do a Google search for "Sabrina adoption" and the city in which we'd lived when we were a foster family.

After scrolling through a couple of pages of results, I stumbled upon a 2002 information request from someone named Kellie, whose original name was, in fact, Sabrina when she'd been adopted more than thirty years prior. Surely this was not possible. Surely I didn't just find someone based only on a first name and location?

Now, having another lead, I searched social media, and suddenly found myself staring at a smiling blonde-haired woman whose mouth drooped ever so slightly on the right side. "I think I found her!" I gasped. My wife, Jennifer, who had no idea what I was looking at on my phone, knew right away who I'd found. She'd heard the story of my foster sister time and again since we'd married, and she knew the loss I carried around in my heart.

Feeling like a stalker, I sent this stranger a private message, along with a picture of Sabrina that my mother had sent me. Ninety minutes later I received a message: "Dear Greg. My birth name was, in fact, Sabrina, and the baby in that picture is me."

A month later, I walked into a restaurant 1,200 miles away and hugged that woman, who is now a NICU nurse and saves babies for a living. After more than thirty years, I'd found my long-lost foster sister.

My point in sharing this story is that while we often set out to address very obvious knots in our lives, sometimes there are knots that only God can untie. And often we don't even realize those knots exist. While I had always wondered what happened to that little baby, I never expected to find her. But doing so at the end of that novena was like having one of the biggest weights I've ever carried lifted away. To know she had a good life, to know that she'd been loved, to know she was happy, meant more to me than I can ever adequately explain.

Whether you can specifically pinpoint any particular sources of stress, anxiety, or unhappiness in your life, or if you simply know you're struggling to have peace in today's world, what you're about to read should be considered a strategy to begin untying the knots of your life in a way that cannot be done on our own. What follows are concrete steps for the next nine days that I can promise you will bring more peace into your life.

Throughout this book I've described how my faith informs my life. But let this now be an invitation. I'm assuming that if you made it this far in reading this book, you have some acceptance of the idea of God, even if you don't have a clearly defined relationship with him. But for some of these next ideas, I want you to trust me a bit. The following things I'm going to propose are not just hypothetical concepts, but concrete steps that transformed my life in significant ways. I believe these recommendations will transform your life for the better, as well.

PRAYING TO MARY, UNDOER OF KNOTS

If you have a knot in your life that you've just never been able to overcome, I can't emphasize enough that it's absolutely critical that you pray this novena. It is based on a meditation by Saint Irenaeus, an early Church Father, bishop of Lyons, who was murdered in AD 202. Saint Paul made a connection between Adam and Jesus Christ, calling Jesus the "second Adam." Saint Irenaeus, in turn, made a similar comparison between Eve and Mary. Eve, by her disobedience, tied the knot of disgrace for the human race, while Mary, by her obedience, undid the knot. Mary's role as Undoer of Knots is what lies behind the entire novena.

Here's the plan in a nutshell: Pray a Rosary every day for the next nine days. (If you don't know how to pray the Rosary, instructions can be found in the Appendix.)

When you begin, make the Sign of the Cross and make an Act of Contrition. In other words, ask for pardon for your sins and make a firm promise not to commit them again. One Act of Contrition is: "Oh my God, I am heartily sorry for having offended you. I detest all my sins because I dread the loss of heaven and the pains of hell, but most of all because I offended you, oh my God, who are all good and deserving of all my love. I firmly resolve with the help of your grace to confess my sins, to do penance, and to amend my life. Amen."

Next, pray the first three decades of the Rosary and read the meditation for that day. Then you say the last two decades of the Rosary and pray the Mary, Undoer of Knots prayer recounted in the Appendix. You do this every day for nine consecutive days.

Don't hesitate, don't stop, don't say I'm going to start on Monday; start it today. Nine days from now you will be finished. As you go into this, I strongly encourage you to write down the biggest core problem that you've identified so far, and then begin the novena. This is your first step to undoing the knots in your life. And I highly suspect that once one knot is untied, others will begin to unravel as well.

If you are skeptical and wonder what will happen on that ninth day, the answer might surprise you. Some people have said that throughout the course of the novena they were surprised when other knots they didn't even know existed became evident. Mary took them and untied them almost right before their eyes. Others have said the exact thing that they were praying for was taken care of right there on the spot. Yet others say their knots were even more tightly bound. It often requires patience, persistence, and sometimes even continuing to pray the Rosary on a daily basis, or offering up additional prayers of fasting and almsgiving. I would say that's been the case for me. I have had to pray this novena multiple times over the course of months for particularly troublesome intentions. But what I found is that, each time, God allowed me to experience the affliction of an unanswered prayer so that I could produce greater endurance, have stronger character, and then have greater hope.

Let me say this: These nine days of a novena are not like a diet. It's not like P90X (an exercise regime) where you work out for ninety days and then think that you're done. This is a mission. We are heading out on a mission. When a military combat unit goes to battle, they don't stop after nine days. They might think they are going to finish in nine days, but sometimes it takes longer. They might expect a certain outcome in nine days, but if they don't have the outcome they want, they don't stop. Neither do we. We push through until the mission of untying knots is accomplished.

As you push through, know that God is at work in your life.

And if you are given a clear answer to your prayers, I encourage you to tell others about it. Be a disciple and tell others that Jesus Christ, through his mother Mary, Undoer of Knots, answered your prayer in such a miraculous and wonderful way.

Like a workout plan, diet, career path, or seeking a degree, finding peace often takes persistence and patience in equal doses.

Saint Gregory of Nyssa once wrote: "He who climbs never stops going from beginning to beginning, through beginnings that have no end. He never stops desiring what he already knows."

As we travel along the ribbon of our lives, we're sure to encounter additional knots and snarls. We'll find knots with simple solutions, like those we discussed in the "Emergency Room" chapter. We'll find knots that, while troubling, actually tie us to the need to trust God and rediscover a prayerful relationship in the midst of difficulties, as discussed in Chapter Ten, "Prayer and Other Tools." And we'll certainly encounter knots we don't even realize we have, as well as knots that are more complex and take a long time to find a solution.

Whenever any of these knots enter your life, I encourage you first to go to Jesus through his mother, Mary, Undoer of Knots. Seek guidance and assistance to endure the knots that develop greater character and hope while also seeking their assistance in untying those knots. At the same time, cultivate and care for the identity that God has given you. Strive to replace the stress with more genuine joy and hope.

Ultimately, we are all seeking the grace of peace through the knots we want untied. And with peace, amazingly, we can live with knots and even find joy in them.

This is why the saints could be martyred with smiles on their faces and why families can find joy through illness and loss. Because where there is suffering, so, too, there is grace.

It is my prayer that as you've journeyed through this book with me the grace and joy of God's love has found its way into your heart.

Mary, Undoer of Knots, pray for us.

Appendix

FULL NOVENA TO MARY, UNDOER OF KNOTS

Day 1

1. Make the Sign of the Cross.
2. Say an Act of Contrition. Ask pardon for your sins and make a firm promise not to commit them again.

   Oh my God, I am heartily sorry for having offended you. I detest all my sins because I dread the loss of heaven and the pains of hell. But most of all, because I offended you, O my God, who are all good and deserving of all my love. I firmly resolve, with the help of your grace, to confess my sins, to do penance, and to amend my life. Amen.

3. Say the first three decades of the Rosary.
4. Make the meditation of the day (see below).
5. Say the last two decades of the Rosary.
6. Finish with the Prayer to Our Lady, Undoer of Knots (Page 168).

Meditation for Day 1

Dearest Holy Mother, Most Holy Mary, you undo the knots that suffocate your children, extend your merciful hands to me. I entrust to you today this knot (state it) and all the negative consequences that it provokes in my life. I give you this knot that torments me and makes me unhappy and so impedes me from uniting myself to you and your Son, Jesus, my Savior.

I run to you, Mary, Undoer of Knots, because I trust you, and I know that you never despise a sinning child who comes to ask you for help. I believe that you can undo this knot because Jesus grants you everything. I believe that you want to undo this knot because you are my Mother. I believe that you will do this because you love me with eternal love.

Thank you, Dear Mother.

Mary, Undoer of Knots, pray for me.

The one who seeks grace finds it in Mary's hands.

Novena to Mary, Undoer of Knots

Day 2

1. Make the Sign of the Cross.
2. Say an Act of Contrition. Ask pardon for your sins and make a firm promise not to commit them again.
3. Say the first three decades of the Rosary.
4. Make the meditation of the day.

5. Say the last two decades of the Rosary.
6. Finish with the Prayer to Our Lady, Undoer of Knots.

Meditation for Day 2

Mary, Beloved Mother, channel of all grace, I return to you today my heart, recognizing that I am a sinner in need of your help. Many times I lose the graces you grant me because of my sins of egoism, pride, rancor, and my lack of generosity and humility. I turn to you today, Mary, Undoer of Knots, for you to ask your Son, Jesus, to grant me a pure, divested, humble, and trusting heart. I will live today practicing these virtues and offering you this as a sign of my love for you. I entrust into your hands this knot (state it) which keeps me from reflecting the glory of God.

Mary, Undoer of Knots, pray for me.

Mary offered all the moments of her day to God.

Novena to Mary, Undoer of Knots

Day 3

1. Make the Sign of the Cross.
2. Say an Act of Contrition. Ask pardon for your sins and make a firm promise not to commit them again.
3. Say the first three decades of the Rosary.
4. Make the meditation of the day.

5. Say the last two decades of the Rosary.
6. Finish with the Prayer to Our Lady, Undoer of Knots.

Meditation for Day 3

Meditating Mother, Queen of Heaven, in whose hands the treasures of the King are found, turn your merciful eyes upon me today. I entrust into your holy hands this knot in my life (state it) and all the rancor and resentment it has caused in me. I ask your forgiveness, God the Father, for my sin. Help me now to forgive all the persons who consciously or unconsciously provoked this knot. Give me, also, the grace to forgive me for having provoked this knot. Only in this way can you undo it. Before you, dearest Mother, and in the name of your Son, Jesus, my Savior, who has suffered so many offenses, having been granted forgiveness, I now forgive these persons (name them) and myself, forever. Thank you, Mary, Undoer of Knots, for undoing the knot of rancor in my heart and the knot which I now present to you. Amen.

Mary, Undoer of Knots, pray for me.

Turn to Mary, you who desire grace.

Novena to Mary Undoer of Knots

Day 4

1. Make the Sign of the Cross.

2. Say an Act of Contrition. Ask pardon for your sins and make a firm promise not to commit them again.
3. Say the first three decades of the Rosary.
4. Make the meditation of the day.
5. Say the last two decades of the Rosary.
6. Finish with the Prayer to Our Lady, Undoer of Knots.

Meditation for Day 4

Dearest Holy Mother, you are generous with all who seek you, have mercy on me. I entrust into your hands this knot which robs the peace of my heart, paralyzes my soul, and keeps me from going to my Lord and serving him with my life.

Undo this knot in my love (state it) O Mother, and ask Jesus to heal my paralytic faith which gets downhearted with the stones on the road. Along with you, dearest Mother, may I see these stones as friends. Not murmuring against them anymore but, giving endless thanks for them, may I smile trustingly in your power.

Mary, Undoer of Knots, pray for me.

Mary is the sun and no one is deprived of her warmth.

NOVENA TO MARY, UNDOER OF KNOTS

Day 5

1. Make the Sign of the Cross.
2. Say an Act of Contrition. Ask pardon for your

sins and make a firm promise not to commit them again.

3. Say the first three decades of the Rosary.
4. Make the meditation of the day.
5. Say the last two decades of the Rosary.
6. Finish with the Prayer to Our Lady, Undoer of Knots.

Meditation for Day 5

Mother, Undoer of Knots, generous and compassionate, I come to you today to once again entrust this knot (state it) in my life to you and to ask the divine wisdom to undo, under the light of the Holy Spirit, this snarl of problems. No one ever saw you angry; to the contrary, your words were so charged with sweetness that the Holy Spirit was manifested on your lips. Take away from me the bitterness, anger, and hatred which this knot has caused me. Give me, O dearest Mother, some of the sweetness and wisdom that is all silently reflected in your heart. And just as you were present at Pentecost, ask Jesus to send me a new presence of the Holy Spirit at this moment in my life. Holy Spirit, come upon me!

Mary, Undoer of Knots, pray for me.

Mary, with God, is powerful.

Novena to Mary, Undoer of Knots

Day 6

1. Make the Sign of the Cross.
2. Say an Act of Contrition. Ask pardon for your sins and make a firm promise not to commit them again.
3. Say the first three decades of the Rosary.
4. Make the meditation of the day.
5. Say the last two decades of the Rosary.
6. Finish with the Prayer to Our Lady, Undoer of Knots.

Meditation for Day 6

Queen of Mercy, I entrust to you this knot in my life (state it), and I ask you to give me a heart that is patient until you undo it. Teach me to persevere in the living word of Jesus, in the Eucharist, and the Sacrament of Penance; stay with me and prepare my heart to celebrate with the angels the grace that will be granted to me. Amen! Alleluia!

Mary, Undoer of Knots, pray for me.

You are beautiful, Mary, and there is no stain of sin in you.

Novena to Mary, Undoer of Knots

Day 7

1. Make the Sign of the Cross.
2. Say an Act of Contrition. Ask pardon for your sins and make a firm promise not to commit them again.
3. Say the first three decades of the Rosary.
4. Make the meditation of the day.
5. Say the last two decades of the Rosary.
6. Finish with the Prayer to Our Lady, Undoer of Knots.

Meditation for Day 7

Mother Most Pure, I come to you today to beg you to undo this knot in my life (state it) and free me from the snares of evil. God has granted you great power over all the demons. I renounce all of them today, every connection I have had with them, and I proclaim Jesus as my one and only Lord and Savior. Mary, Undoer of Knots, crush the evil one's head and destroy the traps he has set for me by this knot. Thank you, dearest Mother. Most Precious Blood of Jesus, free me!

Mary, Undoer of Knots, pray for me.

You are the glory of Jerusalem, the joy of our people.

Novena to Mary, Undoer of Knots

Day 8

1. Make the Sign of the Cross.
2. Say an Act of Contrition. Ask pardon for your sins and make a firm promise not to commit them again.
3. Say the first three decades of the Rosary.
4. Make the meditation of the day.
5. Say the last two decades of the Rosary.
6. Finish with the Prayer to Our Lady, Undoer of Knots.

Meditation for Day 8

Virgin Mother of God, overflowing with mercy, have mercy on your child and undo this knot (state it) in my life. I need your visit to my life, like you visited Elizabeth. Bring me Jesus, bring me the Holy Spirit. Teach me to practice the virtues of courage, joyfulness, humility, and faith, and, like Elizabeth, to be filled with the Holy Spirit. Make me joyfully rest on your bosom, Mary. I consecrate you as my mother, queen, and friend. I give you my heart and everything I have (my home and family, my material and spiritual goods). I am yours forever. Put your heart in me so that I can do everything Jesus tells me.

Mary, Undoer of Knots, pray for me.

Let us go, therefore, full of trust, to the throne of grace.

Novena to Mary, Undoer of Knots

Day 9

1. Make the Sign of the Cross.
2. Say an Act of Contrition. Ask pardon for your sins and make a firm promise not to commit them again.
3. Say the first three decades of the Rosary.
4. Make the meditation of the day.
5. Say the last two decades of the Rosary.
6. Finish with the Prayer to Our Lady, Undoer of Knots.

Meditation for Day 9

Most Holy Mary, our Advocate, Undoer of Knots, I come today to thank you for undoing this knot in my life (state it). You know very well the suffering it has caused me. Thank you for coming, Mother, with your long fingers of mercy to dry the tears in my eyes; you receive me in your arms and make it possible for me to receive once again the divine grace.

Mary, Undoer of Knots, dearest Mother, I thank you for undoing the knots in my life. Wrap me in your mantle of love, keep me under your protection, enlighten me with your peace! Amen.

Mary, Undoer of Knots, pray for me.

Prayer to Mary, Undoer of Knots
(Closing Prayer)

Virgin Mary, Mother of fair love, Mother who never refuses to come to the aid of a child in need, Mother whose hands never cease to serve your beloved children because they are moved by the divine love and immense mercy that exists in your heart, cast your compassionate eyes upon me and see the snarl of knots that exist in my life.

You know very well how desperate I am, my pain, and how I am bound by these knots.

Mary, Mother to whom God entrusted the undoing of the knots in the lives of his children, I entrust into your hands the ribbon of my life.

No one, not even the evil one himself, can take it away from your precious care. In your hands there is no knot that cannot be undone.

Powerful Mother, by your grace and intercessory power with your Son and my Liberator, Jesus, take into your hands today this knot (state it). I beg you to undo it for the glory of God, once for all, you are my hope.

O my Lady, you are the only consolation God gives me, the fortification of my feeble strength, the enrichment of my destitution, and with Christ the freedom from my chains. Hear my plea.

Keep me, guide me, protect me, O safe refuge!

Mary, Undoer of Knots, pray for me.

How to Pray the Rosary

1. Make the Sign of the Cross and say the Apostles' Creed.
2. Say the Our Father.
3. Say three Hail Marys.
4. Say the Glory Be.
5. Announce the First Mystery; then say the Our Father.
6. Say ten Hail Marys while meditating on the mystery.
7. Say the Glory Be.
8. Announce the Second Mystery; then say the Our Father. Repeat 6 and 7 and continue with the Third, Fourth, and Fifth Mysteries.
9. Say the Hail, Holy Queen: "Hail, Holy Queen, Mother of Mercy, our life, our sweetness and our hope! To thee do we cry, poor banished children of Eve. To thee do we send up our sighs, mourning and weeping in this valley of tears! Turn, then, O most gracious Advocate, thine eyes of mercy toward us, and after this, our exile, show unto us the blessed fruit of thy womb, Jesus. O clement, O loving, O sweet Virgin Mary."
10. Conclude with the Sign of the Cross.

Mysteries of the Rosary

Joyful Mysteries
1. The Annunciation
2. The Visitation
3. The Nativity
4. The Presentation of Jesus at the Temple
5. The Finding of Jesus in the Temple

Luminous Mysteries
1. The Baptism of Jesus
2. The Wedding at Cana
3. Jesus' Proclamation of the Kingdom of God
4. The Transfiguration
5. The Institution of the Eucharist

Sorrowful Mysteries
1. The Agony in the Garden
2. The Scourging at the Pillar
3. The Crowning with Thorns
4. The Carrying of the Cross
5. The Crucifixion and Death of Our Lord

Glorious Mysteries
1. The Resurrection
2. The Ascension
3. The Descent of the Holy Spirit
4. The Assumption of Mary
5. The Coronation of Mary as Queen of Heaven

CHAPLET OF DIVINE MERCY
(Prayed on a rosary)

1. Begin with the Sign of the Cross, one Our Father, one Hail Mary, and the Apostles' Creed.
2. Then, on the Our Father beads, say the following:

   "Eternal Father, I offer you the Body and Blood, Soul and Divinity of your dearly beloved Son, our Lord Jesus Christ, in atonement for our sins and those of the whole world."

3. On the ten Hail Mary beads, say the following:

   "For the sake of his sorrowful passion, have mercy on us and on the whole world."

   (Repeat steps 2 and 3 for all five decades).

4. Conclude with (three times):

   "Holy God, Holy Mighty One, Holy Immortal One, have mercy on us and on the whole world."

NOVENA PRAYER TO ST. JOSEPH

O St. Joseph, whose protection is so great, so strong, so prompt before the throne of God, I place in you all my interests and desires.

O St. Joseph, assist me by your powerful intercession and obtain for me from your Divine Son all spiritual blessings through Jesus Christ, Our Lord, so that having engaged here below your heavenly power, I may offer my thanksgiving and homage to the most loving of Fathers.

O St. Joseph, I never weary contemplating you and Jesus asleep in your arms; I dare not approach while he reposes near your heart. Press him in my name and kiss his fine head for me, and ask him to return the kiss when I draw my dying breath. Amen.

O St. Joseph, hear my prayers and obtain my petitions. O Saint Joseph, pray for me. [Mention your intention] (http://www.stjosephsite.com/SJS_Ninedays.htm)

PRAYER TO ST. MICHAEL

St. Michael the Archangel,
defend us in battle,
be our protection against the wickedness and snares of
    the devil;
may God rebuke him, we humbly pray;
and do thou, O Prince of the heavenly host,
by the power of God, cast into hell
Satan and all the evil spirits
who prowl through the world seeking the ruin of souls.
Amen.

Prayer of Trust
(Thomas Merton, *Thoughts in Solitude*)

My Lord God, I have no idea where I am going. I do not see the road ahead of me. I cannot know for certain where it will end. Nor do I really know myself, and the fact that I think that I am following your will does not mean that I am actually doing so. But I believe that the desire to please you does, in fact, please you. And I hope I have that desire in all that I am doing. I hope that I will never do anything apart from that desire. And I know that if I do this you will lead me by the right road though I may know nothing about it. Therefore will I trust you always though I may seem to be lost and in the shadow of death. I will not fear, for you are ever with me, and you will never leave me to face my perils alone.

Special Thanks

To the entire team at OSV who waited with superhuman patience as I completed this manuscript, and for their invaluable assistance at fine-tuning it, ripping it apart, and bringing it together in the book you now hold.

Particular thanks goes to Mary Beth Baker and York Young who both exhibited unending patience with my continually delayed deadlines while also having the unenviable task of editing their boss' book and having to pretend to like it even before it was written.

Thanks as well to others at OSV including Tyler Ottinger (who knocked the cover out of the park on the first try); Jill Adamson, Natalie Fisher, and Polly King (for their support and marketing excellence); Bert Ghezzi and Woodeene Koenig-Bricker for their help on the earliest drafts; Joe Wikert, Kyle Hamilton, and the entire senior leadership team for trusting me with this project; and everyone else at Our Sunday Visitor who worked so tirelessly to make this book happen. Your meticulous dedication and service to the Church is inspiring.

I must also thank Msgrs. Thomas Fryar and Edward Buelt, as well as Shirley McDermott, for providing me with the opportunities to originally develop this content and present it to their parishes and staffs.

Additionally, to the several thousand folks who attended or simply downloaded and listened to my retreat and parish missions about being tied in knots, and for sharing with me their own tales of woe and rescue. The community of people who support my wife and me in our podcasting efforts at www.gregandjennifer. com also played a major role over the last couple years in fine-tuning the content of this book.

Last, thanks to my dear friend Eric and sister Kellie for so graciously letting me share our stories with the world.

Made in the USA
Lexington, KY
17 October 2017